Henry David Thoreau,

The Indian

(Joe Polis, the Bear)

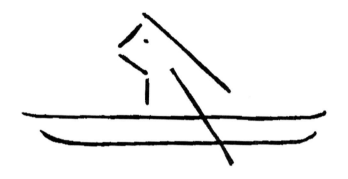

"Great difference between me and white man."

Based on the journal works of:
Henry David Thoreau, The Maine Woods, 1857/1864

2023 ©

Chapters

1. Thoreau's Indian

Joe Polis, the Indian, emerges from Thoreauean history as a guide, an icon, and a man who lived life well, especially in the woods of northern Maine. Now we can study his life with the perspective of time.

Detailed knowledge about Joe Polis comes from the <u>Maine Woods</u> which was skillfully edited and published by Henry David Thoreau's sister, Sophia Elizabeth, in 1864, after Henry's death in 1862. We must all be grateful for Sophia's dedicated work that is seldom heralded. Her book title survives well, as the North woods in Maine is affectionally known simply as The Maine Woods.

Reading the <u>Maine Woods</u>, especially the third section titled the "Allagash and the East Branch", reveals Henry's fascination of exploring anything in the universe that could be studied and squeezed down until it revealed its inner essence (see the story of his fascination with a cold burning light that came out of a smoldering piece of campfire wood), his love of plants and his study of botany along the entire journey, his interest in travel into a changing wilderness and, most powerfully his extensive and perceptive study of his guide, Joseph Polis, a

Penobscot native American. But why did Thoreau repeatedly refer to Joe as "The Indian" * throughout his text? Each reader might form a different answer to this question of naming.

An open-source manuscript of H. D. Thoreau's has been used herein and all text that sheds light on Joe Polis and this wilderness travel, directly or indirectly, has been used with due apologies to all those with a passion for botany! Little has been updated from the original text; changes in style over the last 166 years are obvious and enjoyable. Language has changed! Maps and current photos of places that Thoreau commented on are added.

Henry David Thoreau was born in 1817 and graduated from Yale University in 1837. His liberal arts training served him well as did his close friend, Ralph Waldo Emerson. He identified strongly with Emerson's views on Transcendentalism and contributed greatly to emerging passivism and conscientious objection to many things including taxation, war, slavery, and abuse of the wilderness. He is one of the most noted pioneers in the struggle for wilderness conservation.

---

*Joe Polis is referred to as Mr. Polis once, as Polis 64 times, as Joe 68 times, but in daily direct reference as "the Indian" 257 times in these pages.

Joe Polis is well documented in Thoreau's notes; they are a fascinating record of an amazing man. The record shows a man, Joseph Polis, "the Indian" who was a:

canoe builder,
investor,
entrepreneur,
landowner,
skilled guide across
treacherous waters,
superb navigator,
woodsman,
excellent hunter,
Protestant-Christian,
statesman,
educator,
adviser/consultant and translator,
proprietor of many acres,
worth six thousand dollars,
consultant in Washington.

Thoreau's work consisted of detailed journals that recorded what he keenly observed daily, including three wilderness visits to Maine. His famous book,

Walden, shows his personal traits clearly including his perseverance. He had to self-publish Walden and personally sold copies for $1 apiece. Today it is known worldwide.

But who was Thoreau's Indian? This story can be unfolded now with a retrospective view.

A third person also will be found in this story telling, and that is the present commentator, David Japikse, a licensed Maine Guide, who shall endeavor to give further context by comparing the Polis/Thoreau travels with more recent comments on just how the exploration opened new paths for future generations of wilderness visitation. Hopefully the rigors of the original travel might not be so daunting today.

Joe Polis was a superb guide. Thoreau considered himself lucky to get Joe as his guide. Today it is recognized (by law in Maine) that a guide must guide and with a professional sense of responsibility and training. When hiring a guide, this is to be expected and desired. So, when Henry gets lost on two long portages there is need to examine the root issues, even with a modern perspective that might not be quite applicable back in 1857. Guiding includes various skillsets. There are many guides during the experience of life: every parent is a guide, many civil servants are guides, officers of all types are guides, every worker who has authority over other workers is a guide, clerics are guides; a guide keeps others from getting lost and leads them back if they do get lost. And guides teach a vast variety of skills. Yet, this story almost had a very tragic ending, but for two factors.

This book gives the edited story of Joe Polis, a true wilderness guide, for which the only reference is the Maine Woods. It tells Joe's story and the pursuit of the trip as it was in 1857 and extended to see what a trip in 2023 should be like. Contemporary commentaries are added at the end of each day's entries and further commentary to illustrate a similar trip for modern times is also given.

I hope that you can see an *extremely* talented Penobscot Guide with gifts that rarely can be found today and who serves as an exemplar of superb guiding. Thoreau's writing, when opened up, reveals a powerful study of a fine Penobscot citizen and a Euro American writer in 1857. Readers should be motivated to try parts of this trip and experience the sheer beauty and serenity of this great outdoors!

2. July 20, 1857- Joe Polis, the Bear

The first man we saw on the island was an Indian named Joseph Polis, whom my relative had known from a boy, and now addressed familiarly as "Joe." He was dressing a deer-skin in his yard.

I started on my third excursion to the Maine woods Monday, July 20, 1857, with one companion, arriving at Bangor the next day at noon. We had hardly left the steamer, when we passed Molly Molasses in the street. As long as she lives, the Penobscots may be considered extant as a tribe. The succeeding morning, a relative of mine, who is well acquainted with the Penobscot Indians, and who had been my companion in my two previous excursions into the Maine woods, took me in his wagon to Oldtown, to assist me in obtaining an Indian for this expedition. We were ferried across to the Indian Island in a batteau. The ferryman's boy had got the key to it, but the father, who was a blacksmith, after a little hesitation cut the chain with a cold-chisel on the rock. He told me that the Indians were nearly all gone to the seaboard and to Massachusetts, partly on account of the smallpox—of which they are very much afraid—having broken out in Oldtown, and it was doubtful whether we should find a suitable one at home. The old chief Neptune, however, was there still. The first man we saw on the island was an Indian named Joseph Polis, whom my relative had known from a boy, and now addressed familiarly as "Joe." He was dressing a deer-skin in his yard. The skin was spread over a slanting log, and he was scraping it with a stick held by both hands. He was stoutly built, perhaps a little above the middle height, with a broad face, and, as others said, perfect Indian features and complexion. His house was a two-story white one, with blinds, the best-looking that I noticed there, and as good as an average one on a New England village street. It was surrounded by a garden and fruit-trees, single cornstalks standing thinly amid the beans. We asked him if he knew any good Indian who would like to go into the woods with us, that is, to the Allegash Lakes, by way of Moosehead, and return by the East Branch of the Penobscot, or vary from this as we pleased. To which he answered, out of that strange remoteness in which the Indian ever dwells to the white man, "Me like to go myself; me wants to get some moose;" and kept on scraping the skin. His brother had been into the woods with my relative only a year or two before, and the Indian now inquired what the latter had done to him, that he did not come back, for he had not seen nor heard from him since.

At length we got round to the more interesting topic again. The ferryman had told us that all the best Indians were gone except Polis, who was one of the aristocracy. He to be sure would be the best man we could have, but if he went at all would want a great price; so we did not expect to get him. Polis asked at first two dollars a day, but agreed to go for a dollar and a half, and fifty cents a week for his canoe. He would come to Bangor with his canoe by the seven o'clock train that evening,—we might depend on him. We thought ourselves lucky to secure the services of this man, who was known to be particularly steady and trustworthy.

I spent the afternoon with my companion, who had remained in Bangor, in preparing for our expedition, purchasing provisions, hard-bread, pork, coffee, sugar, etc., and some India-rubber clothing.

We had at first thought of exploring the St. John from its source to its mouth, or else to go up the

Penobscot by its East Branch to the lakes of the St. John, and return by way of Chesuncook and Moosehead. We had finally inclined to the last route, only reversing the order of it, going by way of Moosehead, and returning by the Penobscot, otherwise it would have been all the way upstream and taken twice as long.

At evening the Indian arrived in the cars, and I led the way while he followed me three quarters of a mile to my friend's house, with the canoe on his head. I did not know the exact route myself, but steered by the lay of the land, as I do in Boston, and I tried to enter into conversation with him, but as he was puffing under the weight of his canoe, not having the usual apparatus for carrying it, but, above all, was an Indian, I might as well have been thumping on the bottom of his birch the while. In answer to the various observations which I made by way of breaking the ice, he only grunted vaguely from beneath his canoe once or twice, so that I knew he was there.

Comments:

They set out, Thoreau and his companion on the 20th, arrived on the 21st, and used the 22nd in the company of his relative (cousin or uncle) to make all needed arrangements for the trip in the morning, where they met Joe Polis, and then spent the afternoon in town with his companion. The next morning, the 23rd, they departed by stagecoach.

Polis responded to the invitation to guide the Thoreau trip by saying "Me like to go myself; me wants to get some moose."

Thoreau relates that Joe was at home in a white man's style house (two stories, white, with blinds) of his own, with some affluence. But Polis was always ready to go to the wilderness. And off to the wilderness they went starting by stagecoach. The route is nearly the same today and takes a bit over two hours in light traffic; arriving in one day in 1857 by stagecoach is hard to imagine. Joe was steady and trustworthy, an aristocrat.

The Thoreau-Polis conversations on these first days point to a need for the two men to find a constructive pattern for dialogue and rapport. Chatting while Joe carried the canoe through the town for about ¾ mile was hardly a wise start to conversation. The companion, however, is never identified by name or given a constructive role nor is the "...my friend's house" ever explained. If you, the reader, make a similar trip, you would be wise to choose companions you can communicate with readily and reach compromises and make decisions, as they will surely be needed as nature shows her great variety and intrigue.

3. July 23rd- Traveling

As for the Indian, all the baggage he had, beside his axe and gun, was a blanket, which he brought loose in his hand. However, he had laid in a store of tobacco and a new pipe for the excursion. The canoe was securely lashed diagonally across the top of the stage…

Early the next morning, July 23, the stage called for us, the Indian having breakfasted with us, and already placed the baggage in the canoe to see how it would go. My companion and I had each a large knapsack as full as it would hold, and we had two large india-rubber bags which held our provision and utensils. As for the Indian, all the baggage he had, beside his axe and gun, was a blanket, which he brought loose in his hand. However, he had laid in a store of tobacco and a new pipe for the excursion. The canoe was securely lashed diagonally across the top of the stage, with bits of carpet tucked under the edge to prevent its chafing. The very accommodating driver appeared as much accustomed to carrying canoes in this way as bandboxes.

The Indian sat on the front seat, saying nothing to anybody, with a stolid expression of face, as if barely awake to what was going on. Again I

Fig. 1 Stagecoach and Birch Bark Canoe –
Start of the Travels and Perceptions

was struck by the peculiar vagueness of his replies when addressed in the stage, or at the taverns. He really never said anything on such occasions. He was merely stirred up, like a wild beast, and passively muttered some insignificant response. His answer, in such cases, was never the consequence of a positive mental energy, but vague as a puff of smoke, suggesting no responsibility, and if you considered it, you would find that you had got nothing out of him. This was instead of the conventional palaver and smartness of the white man, and equally profitable. Most get no more than this out of the Indian, and pronounce him stolid accordingly. I was surprised to see what a foolish and impertinent style a Maine man, a passenger, used in addressing him, as if he were a child, which only made his eyes glisten a little. A tipsy

Canadian asked him at a tavern, in a drawling tone, if he smoked, to which he answered with an indefinite "Yes." "Won't you lend me your pipe a little while?" asked the other. He replied, looking straight by the man's head, with a face singularly vacant to all neighboring interests, "Me got no pipe;" yet I had seen him put a new one, with a supply of tobacco, into his pocket that morning.

Our little canoe, so neat and strong, drew a favorable criticism from all the wiseacres among the tavern loungers along the road. By the roadside, close to the wheels, I noticed a splendid great purple fringed orchis with a spike as big as an *Epilobium*, which I would fain have stopped the stage to pluck, but as this had never been known to stop a bear, like the cur on the stage, the driver would probably have thought it a waste of time.

When we reached the lake, about half past eight in the evening, it was still steadily raining, and harder than before; and, in that fresh, cool atmosphere, the hylodes were peeping and the toads ringing about the lake universally, as in the spring with us. It was as if the season had revolved backward two or three months, or I had arrived at the abode of perpetual spring.

We had expected to go upon the lake at once, and, after paddling up two or three miles, to camp on one of its islands; but on account of the steady and increasing rain, we decided to go to one of the taverns for the night, though, for my own part, I should have preferred to camp out.

Comments:

So now we have just met Joe, in a world of his own, desiring to smoke a bit in a quiet refuge, probably as far from the condescending white man, Canadian or not, as possible. And if not condescending, then certainly lacking in understanding of the heritage of the Penobscot people and how to reach within their heart. Polis received several derogatory remarks along the way and was rather annoyed and sullen until they were out on the water on the 24th. Aristocratic, a sharp businessman, at home in the wilderness, while his paying host is seemingly fascinated with the flowers sighted along the road. And it kept raining! How far might these two men go in reaching toward each other?

Travel today to Greenville is different. Steamers no longer arrive in Bangor from Boston, but a swift flight is possible. From Bangor the drive is about 2 hours, but along the same pathway.

4. July 24th - Set for Adventure

I told him that in this voyage I would tell him all I knew, and he should tell me all he knew, to which he readily agreed.

I little thought that there was such a light shining in the darkness of the wilderness for me.

About four o'clock the next morning, though it was quite cloudy, accompanied by the landlord to the water's edge, in the twilight, we launched our canoe from a rock on the Moosehead Lake. When I was there four years before, we had a rather small canoe for three persons, and I had

Fig. 2. An evocation of the outfitting, to scale; Polis in the stern, Thoreau in the bow and companion amidships; each item in the canoe is mentioned in the text but likely larger in size since they were evidently more cramped. Eleven days in an 18' canoe.

thought that this time I would get a larger one, but the present one was even smaller than that. It was 18¼ feet long by 2 feet 6½ inches wide in the middle, and one foot deep within, so I found by measurement, and I judged that it would weigh not far from eighty pounds. The Indian had recently made it himself, and its smallness was partly compensated for by its newness, as well as stanchness and solidity, it being made of very thick bark and ribs. Our baggage weighed about 166 pounds, so that the canoe carried about 600 pounds in all, or the weight of four men (see Figure 2). The principal part of the baggage was, as usual, placed in the middle of the broadest part, while we stowed ourselves in the chinks and crannies that were left before and behind it, where there was no room to extend our legs, the loose articles being tucked into the ends. The canoe was thus as closely packed as a market-basket, and might possibly have been upset without spilling any of its contents. The Indian sat on a cross-bar in the stern, but we flat on the bottom, with a splint or chip behind our backs, to protect them from the cross-bar, and one of us commonly paddled with the Indian. He foresaw that we should not want a pole till we reached the Umbazookskus River, it being either deadwater or down-stream so far, and he was prepared to make a sail of his blanket in the bows if the wind should be fair; but we never used it.

It had rained more or less the four previous days, so that we thought we might count on some fair weather. The wind was at first southwesterly.

Paddling along the eastern side of the lake in the still of the morning, we soon saw a few sheldrakes, which the Indian called Shecorways, and some peetweets, Naramekechus, on the rocky shore; we also saw and heard loons, Medawisla, which he said was a sign of wind. It was inspiriting to hear the regular dip of the paddles, as if they were our fins or flippers, and to realize that we were at length fairly embarked. We who had felt strangely as stage-passengers and tavern-lodgers were suddenly naturalized there and presented with the freedom of the lakes and the woods. Having passed the small rocky isles within two or three miles of the foot of the lake, we had a short consultation respecting our course, and inclined to the western shore for the sake of its lee; for otherwise, if the wind should rise, it would be impossible for us to reach Mount Kineo, which is about midway up the lake on the east side, but at its narrowest part, where probably we could recross if we took the western side. The wind is the chief obstacle to crossing the lakes, especially in so small a canoe. The Indian remarked several times that he did not like to cross the lakes "in littlum canoe," but nevertheless, "just as we say, it made no odds to him." He sometimes took a straight course up the middle of the lake between Sugar and Deer islands, when there was no wind.

Measured on the map, Moosehead Lake is twelve miles wide at the widest place, and thirty miles long in a direct line, but longer as it lies. The captain of the steamer called it thirty-eight miles as he steered. We should probably go about forty. The Indian said that it was called "Mspame, because large water." Squaw Mountain rose darkly on our left, near the outlet of the Kennebec, and what the Indian called Spencer Bay Mountain, on the east, and already we saw Mount Kineo before us in the north.

Paddling near the shore, we frequently heard the *pe-pe* of the olive-sided flycatcher, also the wood pewee, and the kingfisher, thus early in the morning. The Indian reminding us that he could not work without eating, we stopped to breakfast on the main shore, southwest of Deer

Island, at a spot where the Mimulus ringens grew abundantly. We took out our bags, and the Indian made a fire under a very large bleached log, using white pinebark from a stump, though he said that hemlock was better, and kindling with canoe birch bark. Our table was a large piece of freshly peeled birch bark, laid wrong side up, and our breakfast consisted of hard-bread, fried pork, and strong coffee, well sweetened, in which we did not miss the milk.

While we were getting breakfast, a brood of twelve black dippers, half grown, came paddling by within three or four rods, not at all alarmed; and they loitered about as long as we stayed, now huddled close together, within a circle of eighteen inches in diameter, now moving off in a long line, very cunningly. Yet they bore a certain proportion to the great Moosehead Lake on whose bosom they floated, and I felt as if they were under its protection.

Looking northward from this place it appeared as if we were entering a large bay, and we did not know whether we should be obliged to diverge from our course and keep outside a point which we saw, or should find a passage between this and the mainland. I consulted my map and used my glass, and the Indian did the same, but we could not find our place exactly on the map, nor could we detect any break in the shore. When I asked the Indian the way, he answered, "I don't know," which I thought remarkable, since he had said that he was familiar with the lake; but it appeared that he had never been up this side. It was misty dog-day weather, and we had already penetrated a smaller bay of the same kind, and knocked the bottom out of it, though we had been obliged to pass over a small bar, between an island and the shore, where there was but just breadth and depth enough to float the canoe, and the Indian had observed, "Very easy makum bridge here," but now it seemed that, if we held on, we should be fairly embayed. Presently, however, though we had not stirred, the mist lifted somewhat, and revealed a break in the shore northward, showing that the point was a portion of Deer Island, and that our course lay westward of it. Where it had seemed a continuous shore even through a glass, one portion was now seen by the naked eye to be much more distant than the other which overlapped it, merely by the greater thickness of the mist which still rested on it, while the nearer or island portion was comparatively bare and green. The line of separation was very distinct, and the Indian immediately remarked, "I guess you and I go there,—I guess there's room for my canoe there." This was his common expression instead of saying "we." He never addressed us by our names, though curious to know how they were spelled and what they meant, while we called him Polis. He had already guessed very accurately at our ages, and said that he was forty-eight.

After breakfast I, Henry, emptied the melted pork that was left into the lake, making what sailors call a "slick," and watching to see how much it spread over and smoothed the agitated surface. The Indian looked at it a moment and said, "That make hard paddlum thro'; hold 'em canoe. So say old times."

We hastily reloaded, putting the dishes loose in the bows, that they might be at hand when wanted, and set out again. The western shore, near which we paddled along, rose gently to a considerable height, and was everywhere densely covered with the forest, in which was a large proportion of hard wood to enliven and relieve the fir and spruce.

The Indian said that the usnea lichen which we

saw hanging from the trees was called chorchorque. We asked him the names of several small birds which we heard this morning. The wood thrush, which was quite common, and whose note he imitated, he said was called Adelungquamooktum; but sometimes he could not tell the name of some small bird which I heard and knew, but he said, "I tell all the birds about here,—this country; can't tell littlum noise, but I see 'em, then I can tell."

I observed that I should like to go to school to him to learn his language, living on the Indian island the while; could not that be done? "Oh, yer," he replied, "good many do so." I asked how long he thought it would take. He said one week. I told him that in this voyage I would tell him all I knew, and he should tell me all he knew, to which he readily agreed.

The birds sang quite as in our woods,—the red-eye, redstart, veery, wood pewee, etc., but we saw no bluebirds in all our journey, and several told me in Bangor that they had not the bluebird there. Mount Kineo, which was generally visible, though occasionally concealed by islands or the mainland in front, had a level bar of cloud concealing its summit, and all the mountain-tops about the lake were cut off at the same height. Ducks of various kinds— sheldrake, summer ducks, etc.—were quite common, and ran over the water before us as fast as a horse trots. Thus they were soon out of sight.

The Indian asked the meaning of reality, as near as I could make out the word, which he said one of us had used; also of "interrent," that is, intelligent. I observed that he could rarely sound the letter r, but used l, as also r for l sometimes; as load for road, pickelel for pickerel, Soogle Island for Sugar Island, lock for rock, etc. Yet he trilled the r pretty well after me.

I asked him the meaning of the word Musketicook, the Indian name of Concord River. He pronounced it Muskéeticook, emphasizing the second syllable with a peculiar guttural sound, and said that it meant "deadwater," which it is, and in this definition he agreed exactly with the St. Francis Indian with whom I talked in 1853.

The Indian was always very careful in approaching the shore, lest he should injure his canoe on the rocks, letting it swing round slowly side-wise, and was still more particular that we should not step into it on shore, nor till it floated free, and then should step gently lest we should open its seams, or make a hole in the bottom. He said that he would tell us when to jump.

Soon after leaving this point we

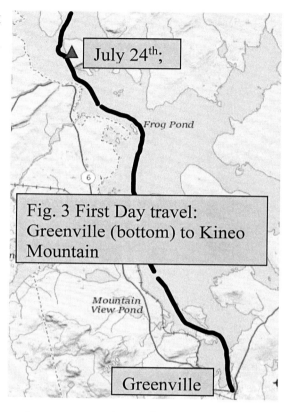

July 24th;

Frog Pond

Fig. 3 First Day travel: Greenville (bottom) to Kineo Mountain

Mountain View Pond

Greenville

passed the Kennebec, or outlet of the lake, and heard the falls at the dam there, for even Moosehead Lake is dammed. After passing Deer Island, we saw the little steamer from Greenville, far east in the middle of the lake, and she appeared nearly stationary. Sometimes we could hardly tell her from an island which had a few trees on it. Here we were exposed to the wind from over the whole breadth of the lake, and ran a little risk of being swamped. While I had my eye fixed on the spot where a large fish had leaped, we took in a gallon or two of water, which filled my lap; but we soon reached the shore and took the canoe over the bar, at Sand-bar Island, a few feet wide only, and so saved a considerable distance. One landed first at a more sheltered place, and walking round caught the canoe by the prow, to prevent it being injured against the shore.

Again we crossed a broad bay opposite the mouth of Moose River, before reaching the narrow strait at Mount Kineo, made what the voyageurs call a traverse, and found the water quite rough. A very little wind on these broad lakes raises a sea which will swamp a canoe. Looking off from the shore, the surface may appear to be very little agitated, almost smooth, a mile distant, or if you see a few white crests they appear nearly level with the rest of the lake; but when you get out so far, you may find quite a sea running, and ere long, before you think of it, a wave will gently creep up the side of the canoe and fill your lap, like a monster deliberately covering you with its slime before it swallows you, or it will strike the canoe violently, and break into it. The same thing may happen when the wind rises suddenly, though it were perfectly calm and smooth there a few minutes before; so that nothing can save you, unless you can swim ashore, for it is impossible to get into a canoe again when it is upset. Since you sit flat on the bottom, though the danger should not be imminent, a little water is a great inconvenience, not to mention the wetting of your provisions. We rarely crossed even a bay directly, from point to point, when there was wind, but made a slight curve corresponding somewhat to the shore, that we might the sooner reach it if the wind increased.

When the wind is aft, and not too strong, the Indian makes a spritsail of his blanket. He thus easily skims over the whole length of this lake in a day.

The Indian paddled on one side, and one of us on the other, to keep the canoe steady, and when he wanted to change hands he would say, "T' other side." He asserted, in answer to our questions, that he had never upset a canoe himself, though he may have been upset by others.

Think of our little eggshell of a canoe tossing across that great lake, a mere black speck to the eagle soaring above it!

My companion trailed for trout as we paddled along, but the Indian warning him that a big fish might upset us, for there are some very large ones there, he agreed to pass the line quickly to him in the stern if he had a bite. Besides trout, I heard of cusk, whitefish, etc., as found in this lake.

While we were crossing this bay, where Mount Kineo rose dark before us, within two or three miles, the Indian repeated the tradition respecting this mountain's having anciently been a cow moose,—how a mighty Indian hunter, whose name I forget, succeeded in killing this queen of the moose tribe with great difficulty, while her calf was killed somewhere among the islands in Penobscot Bay, and, to his eyes, this mountain had still the form of the moose in a reclining posture, its precipitous side presenting the outline of her head. He told this at some length, though it did not amount to much, and with apparent good faith, and asked us how we supposed the hunter could have killed such a mighty moose as that,—how we could do it. Whereupon a man-of-war to fire broadsides into her was suggested, etc. An Indian tells such a story as if he thought it deserved to have a good deal said about it, only he has not got it to say, and so he makes up for the deficiency by a drawling tone, long-windedness, and a dumb wonder which he hopes will be contagious.

We approached the land again through pretty rough water, and then steered directly across the lake, at its narrowest part, to the eastern side, and were soon partly under the lee of the mountain, about a mile north of the Kineo House, having paddled about twenty miles. It was now about noon.

We designed to stop there that afternoon and night, and spent half an hour looking along the shore northward for a suitable place to camp. We took out all our baggage at one place in vain, it being too rocky and uneven, and while engaged in this search we made our first acquaintance with the moose-fly. At length, half a mile farther north, by going half a dozen rods into the dense spruce and fir wood on the side of the mountain, almost as dark as a cellar, we found a place sufficiently clear and level to lie down on, after cutting away a few bushes. We required a space only seven feet by six for our bed, the fire being four or five feet in front, though it made no odds how rough the hearth was; but it was not always easy to find this in those woods. The Indian first cleared a path to it from the shore with his axe, and we then carried up all our baggage, pitched our tent, and made our bed, in order to be ready for foul weather, which then threatened us, and for the night. He gathered a large armful of fir twigs, breaking them off, which he said were the best for our bed, partly, I thought, because they were the largest and could be most rapidly collected. It had been raining more or less for four or five days, and the wood was even damper than usual, but he got dry bark for the fire from the under side of a dead leaning hemlock, which, he said, he could always do.

This noon his mind was occupied with a law question, and I referred him to my companion, who was a lawyer. It appeared that he had been buying land lately (I think it was a hundred acres), but there was probably an incumbrance to it, somebody else claiming to have bought some grass on it for this year. He wished to know to whom the grass belonged, and was told that if the other man could prove that he bought the grass before he, Polis, bought the land, the former could take it, whether the latter knew it or not. To which he only answered, "Strange!" He went over this several times, fairly sat down to it, with his back to a tree, as if he meant to confine us to this topic henceforth; but as he made no headway, only reached the jumping-off place of his wonder at white men's institutions after each explanation, we let the subject die.

He said that he had fifty acres of grass, potatoes, etc., somewhere above Oldtown, besides some about his house; that he hired a good deal of his work, hoeing, etc., and preferred white men to Indians, because "they keep steady, and know how."

After dinner we returned southward along the shore, in the canoe, on account of the difficulty of climbing over the rocks and fallen trees, and began to ascend the mountain along the edge of the precipice. But a smart shower coming up just then, the Indian crept under his canoe, while we, being protected by our rubber coats, proceeded to botanize. So we sent him back to the camp for shelter, agreeing that he should come there for us with his canoe toward night. It had rained a little in the forenoon, and we trusted that this would be the clearing-up shower, which it proved; but our feet and legs were thoroughly wet by the bushes. The clouds breaking away a little, we had a glorious wild view, as we ascended, of the broad lake with its fluctuating surface and numerous forest-clad islands, extending beyond our sight both north and south, and the boundless forest undulating away from its shores on every side, as densely packed as a rye-field, and enveloping nameless mountains in succession; but above all, looking westward over a large island, was visible a very distant part of the lake, though we did not then suspect it to be Moosehead,—at first a mere broken white line seen through the tops of the island trees, like hay-caps, but spreading to a lake when we got higher. Beyond this we saw what appears to be called Bald Mountain on the map, some twenty-five miles distant, near the sources of the Penobscot. It was a perfect lake of the woods. But this was only a transient gleam, for the rain was not quite over.

Looking southward, the heavens were completely overcast, the mountains capped with clouds, and the lake generally wore a dark and stormy appearance, but from its surface just north of Sugar Island, six or eight miles distant, there was reflected upward to us through the misty air a bright blue tinge from the distant unseen sky of another latitude beyond. They probably had a clear sky then at Greenville, the south end of the lake. Standing on a mountain in the midst of a lake, where would you look for the first sign of approaching fair weather? Not into the heavens, it seems, but into the lake.

Again we mistook a little rocky islet seen through the "drisk," with some taller bare trunks or stumps on it, for the steamer with its smoke-pipes, but as it had not changed its position after half an hour, we were undeceived. So much do the works of man resemble the works of nature. A moose might mistake a steamer for a floating isle, and not be scared till he heard its puffing or its whistle.

If I wished to see a mountain or other scenery under the most favorable auspices, I would go to it in foul weather, so as to be there when it cleared up; we are then in the most suitable mood, and nature is most fresh and inspiring. There is no serenity so fair as that which is just established in a tearful eye.

Jackson, in his *Report on the Geology of Maine*, in 1838, says of this mountain: "Hornstone, which will answer for flints, occurs in various parts of the State, where trap-rocks have acted upon silicious slate. The largest mass of this stone known in the world is Mount Kineo, upon Moosehead Lake, which appears to be entirely composed of it, and rises seven hundred feet above the lake level. This variety of hornstone I have seen in every part of New England in the form of Indian arrowheads, hatchets, chisels, etc., which were probably obtained from this mountain by the aboriginal inhabitants of the country." I have myself found hundreds of arrowheads made of the same material. It is generally slate-colored, with white specks, becoming a uniform white where exposed to the light and air, and it breaks with a conchoidal fracture, producing a ragged cutting edge. I noticed some conchoidal hollows more than a foot in diameter. I picked up a small thin piece which had so sharp an edge that I used it as a dull knife, and to see what I could do, fairly cut off an aspen one inch thick with it, by bending it and making many cuts; though I cut my fingers badly with the back of it in the meanwhile.

We met the Indian, puffing and panting, about one third of the way up, but thinking that he must be near the top, and saying that it took his breath away. I thought that superstition had something to do with his fatigue. Perhaps he believed that he was climbing over the back of a tremendous moose. He said that he had never ascended Kineo. On reaching the canoe we found that he had caught a lake trout weighing about three pounds, at the depth of twenty-five or thirty feet, while we were on the mountain.

When we got to the camp, the canoe was taken out and turned over, and a log laid across it to prevent its being blown away. The Indian cut some large logs of damp and rotten hard wood to smoulder and keep fire through the night. The trout was fried for supper. Our tent was of thin cotton cloth and quite small, forming with the ground a triangular prism closed at the rear end, six feet long, seven wide, and four high, so that we could barely sit up in the middle. It required two forked stakes, a smooth ridge-pole, and a dozen or more pins to pitch it. It kept off dew and wind, and an ordinary rain, and answered our purpose well enough. We reclined within it till bedtime, each with his baggage at his head, or else sat about the fire, having hung our wet clothes on a pole before the fire for the night.

As we sat there, just before night, looking out through the dusky wood, the Indian heard a noise which he said was made by a snake. He imitated it at my request, making a low whistling note,—pheet—pheet,—two or three times repeated, somewhat like the peep of the hylodes, but not so loud. In answer to my inquiries, he said that he had never seen them while making it, but going to the spot he finds the snake. This, he said on another occasion, was a sign of rain. When I had selected this place for our camp, he had remarked that there were snakes there,—he saw them. "But they won't do any hurt," I said. "Oh, no," he answered, "just as you say; it makes no difference to me."

He lay on the right side of the tent, because, as he said, he was partly deaf in one ear, and he wanted to lie with his good ear up. As we lay there, he inquired if I ever heard "Indian sing." I replied that I had not often, and asked him if he would not favor us with a song. He readily assented, and, lying on his back, with his blanket wrapped around him, he commenced a slow, somewhat nasal, yet musical chant, in his own language, which probably was taught his tribe long ago by the Catholic missionaries. He translated it to us, sentence by sentence, afterward, wishing to see if we could remember it. It proved to be a very simple religious exercise or hymn, the burden of which was, that there was only one God who ruled all the world. This was hammered (or sung) out very thin, so that some stanzas well-nigh meant nothing at all, merely keeping up the idea. He then said that he would sing us a Latin song; but we did not detect any Latin, only one or two Greek words in it,—the rest may have been Latin with the Indian pronunciation.

His singing carried me back to the period of the discovery of America, to San Salvador and the Incas, when Europeans first encountered the simple faith of the Indian. There was, indeed, a beautiful simplicity about it; nothing of the dark and savage, only the mild and infantile. The sentiments of humility and reverence chiefly were expressed.

It was a dense and damp spruce and fir wood in which we lay, and, except for our fire, perfectly dark; and when I awoke in the night, I either heard an owl from deeper in the forest behind us, or a loon from a distance over the lake. Getting up some time after midnight to collect the scattered brands together, while my companions were sound asleep, I observed, partly in the fire, which had ceased to blaze, a perfectly regular elliptical ring of light, about five inches in its shortest diameter, six or seven in its longer, and from one eighth to one quarter of an inch wide. It was fully as bright as the fire, but not reddish or scarlet, like a coal, but a white and slumbering light, like the glow-worm's. I could tell it from the fire only by its whiteness. I saw at once that it must be phosphorescent wood, which I had so often heard of, but never chanced to see. Putting my finger on it, with a little hesitation, I found that it was a piece of dead moose-wood (*Acer striatum*) which the Indian had cut off in a slanting direction the evening before. Using my knife, I discovered that the light proceeded from that portion of the sap-wood immediately under the bark, and thus presented a regular ring at the end, which, indeed, appeared raised above the level of the wood, and when I pared off the bark and cut into the sap, it was all aglow along the log. I was surprised to find the wood quite hard and apparently sound, though probably decay had commenced in the sap, and I cut out some little triangular chips, and, placing them in the hollow of my hand, carried them into the camp, waked my companion, and showed them to him. They lit up the inside of my hand, revealing the lines and wrinkles, and appearing exactly like coals of fire raised to a white heat, and I saw at once how, probably, the Indian jugglers had imposed on their people and on travelers, pretending to hold coals of fire in their mouths.

I also noticed that part of a decayed stump within four or five feet of the fire, an inch wide and six inches long, soft and shaking wood, shone with equal brightness.

I neglected to ascertain whether our fire had anything to do with this, but the previous day's rain and long-continued wet weather undoubtedly had.

I was exceedingly interested by this phenomenon, and already felt paid for my journey. It could hardly have thrilled me more if it had taken the form of letters, or of the human face. If I had met with this ring of light while groping in this forest alone, away from any fire, I should have been still more surprised. I little thought that there was such a light shining in the darkness of the wilderness for me.

The next day the Indian told me their name for this light,—artoosoqu'—and on my inquiring concerning the will-o'-the-wisp, and the like phenomena, he said that his "folks" sometimes saw fires passing along at various heights, even as high as the trees, and making a noise. I was prepared after this to hear of the most startling and unimagined phenomena, witnessed by "his folks;" they are abroad at all hours and seasons in scenes so unfrequented by white men. Nature must have made a thousand revelations to them which are still secrets to us.

I did not regret my not having seen this before, since I now saw it under circumstances so favorable. I was in just the frame of mind to see something wonderful, and this was a phenomenon adequate to my circumstances and expectation, and it put me on the alert to see more like it. I exulted like "a pagan suckled in a creed" that had never been worn at all, but was brand-new, and adequate to the occasion. I let science slide, and rejoiced in that light as if it had been a fellow creature. I saw that it was excellent, and was very glad to know that it was so cheap. A scientific explanation, as it is called, would have been altogether out of place there. That is for pale daylight. Science with its retorts would have put me to sleep; it was the opportunity to be ignorant that I improved. It suggested to me that there was something to be seen if one had eyes. It made a believer of me more than before. I believed that the woods were not tenantless, but choke-full of honest spirits as good as myself any day, —not an empty chamber, in which chemistry was left to work alone, but an inhabited house,—and for a few moments I enjoyed fellowship with them. Your so-called wise man goes trying to persuade himself that there is no entity there but himself and his traps, but it is a great deal easier to believe the truth. It suggested, too, that the same experience always gives birth to the same sort of belief or religion. One revelation has been made to the Indian, another to the white man. I have much to learn of the Indian, nothing of the missionary. I am not sure but all that would tempt me to teach the Indian my religion would be his promise to teach me his. Long enough I had heard of irrelevant things; now at length I was glad to make acquaintance with the light that dwells in rotten wood. Where is all your knowledge gone to? It evaporates completely, for it has no depth.

Comments:

A degree of socializing hence began and while Thoreau knew of Joe Polis as "Joe" from his relative's familiarity with him since boyhood, nevertheless he decided to call him Polis, which is far better than the "companion" who remained nameless throughout the entire experience even though Henry desired to bring him along on the trip! It is curious, though, that in the writing, Henry almost always referred to Polis as "the Indian," which could fall short of the full character that Joe Polis had attained with his life in the wilderness, which is a stern but passionate teacher, as well as in the cities and byways of the east.

In a brief time, the socializing took a turn to a deeper relationship and a sort of contract to share learning, if not wisdom, was reached to end only at a distant junction.

Henry's description of Moosehead Lake and the dangers of stormy weather are very accurate and his commentary is highly relevant today. It is instructive to compare the birch bark canoe with today's modern canoe, which gives much credit to the original native construction of their invention. Many types of canoes are available today but hold few advantages to the one that Thoreau used with Joe Polis. Perhaps the one disadvantage is the need to carefully place ones footing so as not to punch through the bark, which apparently never happened on Henry's trips. This canoe was a good size compared with appropriate canoes for similar travel today. Of course, seats were greatly improved with time. Both canoes in Henry's writings apparently were built with a very straight heading, at least no mention was every made of a tendency for the canoe to head off to either side. This is amazing since there isn't any formal laying of the keel, and in fact there is none in the birch bark canoe construction. These canoes were economical, sufficiently durable, seaworthy, reparable, and light enough for the carry. They made very good time from Greenville to Kineo, about half a day for about 20 miles, which was facilitated by some favorable wind from time to time.

Being out on the waters and enjoying the solitude of nature is well know as restorative; when the three of them got out on that first morning, Thoreau remarked that they "...were suddenly naturalized there and presented with the freedom of the lakes and the woods."

So Joe, as canoe builder, investor, entrepreneur, land owner and skilled guide across treacherous waters begins to emerge, even though still referred to as "the Indian."

Thoreau states that it is impossible to re-enter a canoe once it has gone over. Truly, it is VERY difficult, but not impossible. As a youth, this writer had to demonstrate proficiency in handling a swamped canoe and paddling it onwards. But this is done with an otherwise empty canoe in warm *weather without strong winds. It can still be done, but the risk is very high and may not be successful, often leading to drowning. It is far better to have at least two canoes on a trip so that one can give proper assistance to the other.*

Resting at nighttime, Henry David Thoreau has experienced just one of countless marvels to be found in the great wilderness. He even professes,

> *I let science slide, and rejoiced in that light as if it had been a fellow creature. I saw that it was excellent, and was very glad to know that it was so cheap. A scientific explanation, as it is called, would have been altogether out of place there. That is for pale daylight. Science with its retorts would have put me to sleep; it was the opportunity to be ignorant that I improved. It suggested to me that there was something to be seen if one had eyes. It made a believer of me more than before. I believed that the woods were not tenantless, but choke-full of honest spirits as good as myself any day, —not an empty chamber, in which chemistry was left to work alone, but an inhabited house,—and for a few moments I enjoyed fellowship with them. Your so-called wise man goes trying to persuade himself that there is no entity there but himself and his traps, but it is a great deal easier to believe the truth.*

This is one of many epiphanies that Thoreau strikes upon as he kept his lifelong journal, from which grew various books, social movements, and deep philosophies. How wonderful to experience a new phenomenon with the fresh joy even as that of a little child. But then he ceases being the unbridled observer and adopts the biased view of one who must defend the presumed solid facts of the day:

> *Your so-called wise man goes trying to persuade himself that there is no entity there but himself and his traps, but it is a great deal easier to believe the truth. It suggested, too, that the same experience always gives birth to the same sort of belief or religion. One revelation has been made to the Indian, another to the white man. I have much to learn of the Indian, nothing of the missionary. I am not sure but all that would tempt me to teach the Indian my religion would be his promise to teach me his. Long enough I had heard of irrelevant things; now at length I was glad to make acquaintance with the light that dwells in rotten wood. Where is all your knowledge gone to? It evaporates completely, for it has no depth.*

He starts this passage very well indeed but aids his reader not at all as he shifts to a discourse on religion, a subject that seems to have troubled or challenged him all his life long. And then he continues:

> *I kept those little chips and wet them again the next night, but they emitted no light.*

... they emitted no light." Is that profound or misguided?

5. *Vignette 1:* Making a Fire

Having spent a number of years as a Scoutmaster and starting each new crop of young scouts towards their Tenderfoot rank, I have often taught lads on how to make a fire. The first group that I taught had to learn just after a deluge from the sky and many complaints were lodged on the impossibility of making the fire and how unfair it was. They all made a fire that day with no artificial means and just two matches. Many of them went on to become Eagle scouts!

Thoreau shares a few hints of how to do this (usually after a rain):

> …and the Indian made a fire under a very large bleached log, using white pine bark from a stump, though he said that hemlock was better, and kindling with canoe birch bark.

> It had been raining more or less for four or five days, and the wood was even damper than usual, but he got dry bark for the fire from the under side of a dead leaning hemlock, which, he said, he could always do.

Elsewhere in his text, he mentions using other barks and his strong preference for using hard wood for cooking meat over an open fire. Many other techniques are known and can be read about. In the Maine woods, due to continued harvesting of trees and their regrowth, there is competition from larger and smaller trees with many of the latter dying off but taking years to fall over. Even in a rainstorm, many of these smaller trees have a dry side and much of the wood beneath the bark is quite dry and are excellent for starting a fire. (Please do not use birch bark – unless it has naturally fallen on the ground - as it harms a living tree and just is not needed for making our fires.)

Other scout tricks for fire starting are well worth learning: making a fuzz stick, using lint from your pockets, carrying some self-made wax/cardboard fire starters, looking under dead logs (lying near the ground, or hanging at an angle) for dry materials, and so forth. If the reader wishes to start on outdoor travels without a guide, be sure to practice fire starting after a good storm and postpone any trip until you are good at this skill or plan to use bottled fuel.

6. July 25- Great Differences

*Oh, I can't tell you, he replied. Great difference between
me and white man.*

At breakfast this Saturday morning, the Indian, evidently curious to know what would be expected of him the next day, whether we should go along or not, asked me how I spent the Sunday when at home. I told him that I commonly sat in my chamber reading, etc., in the forenoon, and went to walk in the afternoon. At which he shook his head and said, "Er, that is ver bad." "How do you spend it?" I asked. He said that he did no work, that he went to church at Oldtown when he was at home; in short, he did as he had been taught by the whites. This led to a discussion in which I found myself in the minority. He stated that he was a Protestant, and asked me if I was. I did not at first know what to say, but I thought that I could answer with truth that I was.

The weather seemed to be more settled this morning, and we set out early in order to finish our voyage up the lake before the wind arose. Soon after starting, the Indian directed our attention to the Northeast Carry, which we could plainly see, about thirteen miles distant in that direction as measured on the map, though it is called much farther. This carry is a rude wooden railroad, running north and south about two miles, perfectly straight, from the lake to the Penobscot, through a low tract, with a clearing three or four rods wide; but low as it is, it passes over the height of land there. This opening appeared as a clear bright, or light, point in the horizon, resting on the edge of the lake, whose breadth a hair could have covered at a considerable distance from the eye, and of no appreciable height. We should not have suspected it to be visible if the Indian had not drawn our attention to it. It was a remarkable kind of light to steer for,—daylight seen through a vista in the forest,—but visible as far as an ordinary beacon at night.

We crossed a deep and wide bay which makes eastward north of Kineo, leaving an island on our left, and keeping up the eastern side of the lake. This way or that led to some Tomhegan or Socatarian stream, up which the Indian had hunted, and whither I longed to go. The last name, however, had a bogus sound, too much like sectarian for me, as if a missionary had tampered with it; but I knew that the Indians

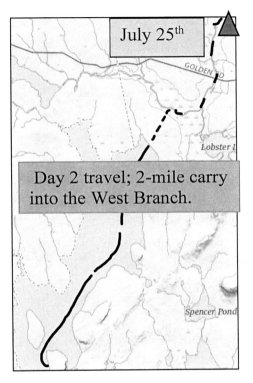

Day 2 travel; 2-mile carry into the West Branch.

Fig.4. North end of Moosehead Lake; strong waves when party crossed.

were very liberal. I think I should have inclined to the Tomhegan first.

We then crossed another broad bay, which, as we could no longer observe the shore particularly, afforded ample time for conversation. The Indian said that he had got his money by hunting, mostly high up the West Branch of the Penobscot, and toward the head of the St. John; he had hunted there from a boy, and knew all about that region. His game had been beaver, otter, black cat (or fisher), sable, moose, etc. Loup-cervier (or Canada lynx) were plenty yet in burnt grounds. For food in the woods, he uses partridges, ducks, dried moose- meat, hedgehog, etc. Loons, too, were good, only "bile 'em good." He told us at some length how he had suffered from starvation when a mere lad, being overtaken by winter when hunting with two grown Indians in the northern part of Maine, and obliged to leave their canoe on account of ice.

Pointing into the bay, he said that it was the way to various lakes which he knew. Only solemn bear-haunted mountains, with their great wooded slopes, were visible; where, as man is not, we suppose some other power to be. My imagination personified the slopes themselves, as if by their very length they would waylay you, and compel you to camp again on them before night. Some invisible glutton would seem to drop from the trees and gnaw at the heart of the solitary hunter who threaded those woods; and yet I was tempted to walk there. The Indian said that he had been along there several times.

I asked him how he guided himself in the woods. "Oh," said he, "I can tell good many ways." When I pressed him further, he answered, "Sometimes I lookum side-hill," and he glanced toward a high hill or mountain on the eastern shore, "great difference between the north and south, see where the sun has shone most. So trees,—the large limbs bend toward south.

Sometimes I lookum locks" (rocks). I asked what he saw on the rocks, but he did not describe anything in particular, answering vaguely, in a mysterious or drawling tone, "Bare locks on lake shore,—great difference between north, south, east, west, side,—can tell what the sun has shone on." "Suppose," said I, "that I should take you in a dark night, right up here into the middle of the woods a hundred miles, set you down, and turn you round quickly twenty times, could you steer straight to Oldtown?" "Oh, yer," said he, "have done pretty much same thing. I will tell you. Some years ago I met an old white hunter at Millinocket; very good hunter. He said he could go anywhere in the woods. He wanted to hunt with me that day, so we start. We chase a moose all the forenoon, round and round, till middle of afternoon, when we kill him. Then I said to him, 'Now you go straight to camp. Don't go round and round where we've been, but go straight.' He said, 'I can't do that, I don't know where I am.' 'Where you think camp?' I asked. He pointed so. Then I laugh at him. I take the lead and go right off the other way, cross our tracks many times, straight camp." "How do you do that?" asked I. "Oh, I can't tell you," he replied. "Great difference between me and white man."

It appeared as if the sources of information were so various that he did not give a distinct, conscious attention to any one, and so could not readily refer to any when questioned about it, but he found his way very much as an animal does. Perhaps what is commonly called instinct in the animal, in this case is merely a sharpened and educated sense. Often, when an Indian says, "I don't know," in regard to the route he is to take, he does not mean what a white man would by those words, for his Indian instinct may tell him still as much as the most confident white man knows. He does not carry things in his head, nor remember the route exactly, like a white man, but relies on himself at the moment. Not having experienced the need of the other sort of knowledge, all labeled and arranged, he has not acquired it.

The white hunter with whom I talked in the stage knew some of the resources of the Indian. He said that he steered by the wind, or by the limbs of the hemlocks, which were largest on the south side; also sometimes, when he knew that there was a lake near, by firing his gun and listening to hear the direction and distance of the echo from over it.

The course we took over this lake, and others afterward, was rarely direct, but a succession of curves from point to point, digressing considerably into each of the bays; and this was not merely on account of the wind, for the Indian, looking toward the middle of the lake, said it was hard to go there, easier to keep near the shore, because he thus got over it by successive reaches and saw by the shore how he got along.

The following will suffice for a common experience in crossing lakes in a canoe. As the forenoon advanced, the wind increased. The last bay which we crossed before reaching the desolate pier at the Northeast Carry was two or three miles over, and the wind was southwesterly. After going a third of the way, the waves had increased so as occasionally to wash into the canoe, and we saw that it was worse and worse ahead. At first we might have turned about, but were not willing to. It would have been of no use to follow the course of the shore, for not only the distance would have been much greater, but the waves ran still higher there on account of the greater sweep the wind had. At any rate it would have been dangerous now to alter our course, because the waves would have struck us at an advantage. It will not do to meet them at right angles, for then they will wash in both sides, but you must take them quartering. So the Indian stood up in the canoe, and exerted all his skill and strength for a mile or two, while I paddled right along in order to give him more steerage-way. For more than a mile he did not allow a single wave to strike the canoe as it would, but turned it quickly from this side to that, so that it would always be on or near the crest of a wave when it broke, where all its force was spent, and we merely settled down with it. At length I jumped out on to the end of the pier, against which the waves were dashing violently, in order to lighten the canoe, and catch it at the landing, which was not much sheltered; but just as I jumped we took in two or three gallons of water. I remarked to the Indian, "You managed that well," to which he replied, "Ver few men do that. Great many waves; when I look out for one, another come quick."

While the Indian went to get cedar bark, etc., to carry his canoe with, we cooked the dinner on the shore, at this end of the carry, in the midst of a sprinkling rain.

He prepared his canoe for carrying in this wise. He took a cedar shingle or splint eighteen inches long and four or five wide, rounded at one end, that the corners might not be in the way, and tied it with cedar bark by two holes made midway, near the edge on each side, to the middle cross-bar of the canoe. When the canoe was lifted upon his head bottom up, this shingle, with its rounded end uppermost, distributed the weight over his shoulders and head, while a band of cedar bark, tied to the cross-bar on each side of the shingle, passed round his breast, and another longer one, outside of the last, round his forehead; also a hand on each side-rail served to steer the canoe and keep it from rocking. He thus carried it with his shoulders, head, breast, forehead, and both hands, as if the upper part of his body were all one hand to clasp and hold it. If you know of a better way, I should like to hear of it. A cedar tree furnished all the gear in this case, as it had the woodwork of the canoe. One of the paddles rested on the cross-bars in the bows. I took the canoe upon my head and found that I could carry it with ease, though the straps were not fitted to my shoulders; but I let him carry it, not caring to establish a different precedent, though he said that if I would carry the canoe, he would take all the rest of the baggage, except my companion's. This shingle remained tied to the cross-bar throughout the voyage, was always ready for the carries, and also served to protect the back of one passenger.

We were obliged to go over this carry twice, our load was so great. But the carries were an agreeable variety, and we improved the opportunity to gather the rare plants which we had seen, when we returned empty handed.

We reached the Penobscot about four o'clock, and found there some St. Francis Indians encamped on the bank, in the same place where I camped with four Indians four years before. They were making a canoe, and, as then, drying moose-meat. The meat looked very suitable to make a blackbroth at least. Our Indian said it was not good. Their camp was covered with spruce bark. They had got a young moose, taken in the river a fortnight before, confined in a sort of cage of logs piled up cob-fashion, seven or eight feet high. It was quite tame, about four feet high, and covered with moose-flies. There was a large quantity of cornel (*C. stolonifera*), red maple, and also willow and aspen boughs, stuck through between the logs on all sides, butt ends out, and on their leaves it was browsing. It looked at first as if it were in a bower rather than a pen.

Our Indian said that he used black spruce roots to sew canoes with, obtaining it from high lands or mountains. The St. Francis Indian thought that white spruce roots might be best. But the former said, "No good, break, can't split 'em;" also that they were hard to get, deep in ground, but the black were near the surface, on higher land, as well as tougher. He said that the white spruce was subekoondark, black, skusk. I told him I thought that I could make a canoe, but he expressed great doubt of it; at any rate, he thought that my work would not be "neat" the first time. An Indian at Greenville had told me that the winter bark, that is, bark taken off before the sap flows in May, was harder and much better than summer bark.

Having reloaded, we paddled down the Penobscot, which, as the Indian remarked, and even I detected, remembering how it looked before, was uncommonly full. We soon after saw a splendid yellow lily (*Lilium Canadense*) by the shore, which I plucked. It was six feet high, and had twelve flowers, in two whorls, forming a pyramid, such as I have seen in Concord. We afterward saw many more thus tall along this stream, and also still more numerous on the East Branch, and, on the latter, one which

I thought approached yet nearer to the *Lilium superbum*. The Indian asked what we called it, and said that the "loots" (roots) were good for soup, that is, to cook with meat, to thicken it, taking the place of flour. They get them in the fall. I dug some, and found a mass of bulbs pretty deep in the earth, two inches in diameter, looking, and even tasting, somewhat like raw green corn on the ear.

When we had gone about three miles down the

Figure 5. West Branch, Penobscot River

Penobscot, we saw through the tree-tops a thunder-shower coming up in the west, and we looked out a camping-place in good season, about five o'clock, on the west side, not far below the mouth of what Joe Aitteon, in '53, called Lobster Stream, coming from Lobster Pond. Our present Indian, however, did not admit this name, nor even that of Matahumkeag, which is on the map, but called the lake Beskabekuk.

I will describe, once for all, the routine of camping at this season. We generally told the Indian that we would stop at the first suitable place, so that he might be on the lookout for it. Having observed a clear, hard, and flat beach to land on, free from mud, and from stones which would injure the canoe, one would run up the bank to see if there were open and level space enough for the camp between the trees, or if it could be easily cleared, preferring at the same time a cool place, on account of insects. Sometimes we paddled a mile or more before finding one to our minds, for where the shore was suitable, the bank would often be too steep, or else too low and grassy, and therefore mosquitoey. We then took out the baggage and drew up the canoe, sometimes turning it over on shore for safety. The Indian cut a path to the spot we had selected, which was usually within two or three rods of the water, and we carried up our baggage. One, perhaps, takes canoe birch bark, always at hand, and dead dry wood or bark, and kindles a fire five or six feet in front of where we intend to lie. It matters not, commonly, on which side this is, because there is little or no wind in so dense a wood at that season; and then he gets a kettle of water from the river, and takes out the pork, bread, coffee, etc., from their several packages.

Another, meanwhile, having the axe, cuts down the nearest dead rock maple or other dry hard wood, collecting several large logs to last through the night, also a green stake, with a notch or fork to it, which is slanted over the fire, perhaps resting on a rock or forked stake, to hang the kettle on, and two forked stakes and a pole for the tent.

The third man pitches the tent, cuts a dozen or more pins with his knife, usually of moose-wood, the common underwood, to fasten it down with, and then collects an armful or two of fir twigs, arbor-vitæ, spruce, or hemlock, whichever is at hand, and makes the bed, beginning at either end, and laying the twigs wrong side up, in regular rows, covering the stub ends of the last row; first, however, filling the hollows, if there are any, with coarser material. Wrangel says that his guides in Siberia first strewed a quantity of dry brushwood on the ground, and then cedar twigs on that.

Commonly, by the time the bed is made, or within fifteen or twenty minutes, the water boils, the pork is fried, and supper is ready. We eat this sitting on the ground, or a stump, if there is any, around a large piece of birch bark for a table, each holding a dipper in one hand and a piece of ship-bread or fried pork in the other, frequently making a pass with his hand, or thrusting his head into the smoke, to avoid the mosquitoes.

Next, pipes are lit by those who smoke, and veils are donned by those who have them, and we hastily examine and dry our plants, anoint our faces and hands, and go to bed—and—the mosquitoes.

Though you have nothing to do but see the country, there's rarely any time to spare, hardly enough to examine a plant, before the night or drowsiness is upon you.

Such was the ordinary experience, but this evening we had camped earlier on account of the rain, and had more time.

Comments:

So we add navigator and woodsman to the impressive vitae *that Joe Polis possessed.*

How ironic that, just after Thoreau sharply criticizes organized religion, or at least missionaries, that he is confronted by "the Indian" and is thoroughly stumped by the question as to his own religion; if one has to think over the question to say that he was truthfully a Protestant, himself, is it perhaps tantamount to being not so at all?

Few accounts of canoeing in rough weather have been so well written and it heralds the amazing skill that Joe Polis possessed. To stand up in a birch bark canoe in a storm has risks to be sure, but to continuously swerve the canoe onto and out of each breaking wave is extraordinary skill especially with a birch bark canoe. He was clearly a very strong man and deeply experienced.

As a rule canoeists stay out of rough water, select the lee side of a lake for protection, do not cross open bays, keep their center of gravity as low as possible in the canoe and prefer to quarter with the wind and keep it as much behind as practical. When possible, it is good to ride the crests as Joe was doing. But to stand up in a canoe in any weather? Risky in most circumstances but done in carefully controlled conditions. This was one of them where Joe knew his skill set, had the strength and balance and knew he could count on his charges to remain steady and well centered in the canoe. Standing up implies very powerful strokes, probably leveraged off the gunwales. His foot did not go through the birch floor or walls and his powerful leveraged strokes did not break the gunwales. So the canoe was very well made indeed. Many of the cheaper modern canoes might not hold up so well.

This standing up paddling perhaps explains the later revelation that Joe used a longer paddle in the stern than his bowman did, which is not the common case today.

But just at the end of the Moosehead lengthwise traverse, a small glitch occurs, and Joe politely does not call out his 'experienced' bowman on it:

> *At length I jumped out on to the end of the pier, against which the waves were dashing violently, in order to lighten the canoe, and catch it at the landing, which was not much sheltered; but just as I jumped we took in two or three gallons of water.*

This glitch often flips the entire canoe and all its goods over into the drink! The operative principle is to load and unload a canoe so as to keep the maximum amount of weight as near the center of the canoe and as low as possible. Hence the center is loaded first and unloaded last, the bow (which is closer to the center than the stern is) is loaded next and unloaded next to last and the stern, which is furthest from the center, is unloaded first and loaded last. If a bowman jumps out first and slightly off center it may well result in a complete bath. In this case, just a few gallons of water spilled in, even though Joe had managed all the high waves without incident.

Just imagine where those two or three gallons of water end up! Since he is pulling the canoe bow up onto the shore, he is lifting that end so the water quickly rolls down the center of the canoe flooding, firstly, his companion with water through his crotch and then on to patient Joe Polis perhaps sitting on a thwart getting only his feet wet (or wetter), or perhaps worse.

Just how experienced was Thoreau?

7. July 26- Caucomgomoctook, Chesuncook, Umbazookskus

He understood very well both his superiority and his inferiority to the whites.

I told the Indian that we would go to church to Chesuncook this morning, some fifteen miles. It was settled weather at last. A few swallows flitted over the water, we heard Maryland yellow-throats along the shore, the phebe

Figure 6. Chesuncook Church, as it is today; accessed by canoe or 4-wheel drive.

notes of the chickadee, and, I believe, redstarts, and moose-flies of large size pursued us in midstream.

The Indian thought that we should lie by on Sunday. Said he, "We come here lookum things, look all round; but come Sunday, lock up all that, and then Monday look again." He spoke of an Indian of his acquaintance who had been with some ministers to Ktaadn, and had told him how they conducted. This he described in a low and solemn voice. "They make a long prayer every morning and night, and at every meal. Come Sunday," said he, "they stop 'em, no go at all that day,—keep still,—preach all day,—first one, then another, just like church. Oh, ver good men." "One day," said he, "going along a river, they came to the body of a man in the water, drowned good while, all ready fall to pieces. They go right ashore,—stop there, go no farther that day,—they have meeting there, preach and pray just like Sunday. Then they get poles and lift up the body, and they go back and carry the body with them. Oh, they ver good men."

I judged from this account that their every camp was a camp-meeting, and they had mistaken their route,—they should have gone to Eastham; that they wanted an opportunity to preach somewhere more than to see Ktaadn. I read of another similar party that seem to have spent their time there singing the songs of Zion. I was glad that I did not go to that mountain with such slow coaches.

However, the Indian added, plying the paddle all the while, that if we would go along, he must go with us, he our man, and he suppose that if he no takum pay for what he do Sunday, then ther's no harm, but if he takum pay, then wrong. I told him that he was stricter than white men. Nevertheless, I noticed that he did not forget to reckon in the Sundays at last.

He appeared to be a very religious man, and said his prayers in a loud voice, in Indian, kneeling before the camp, morning and evening,— sometimes scrambling up again in haste when he had forgotten this, and saying them with great rapidity. In the course of the day, he remarked, not very originally, "Poor man rememberum God more than rich."

We soon passed the island where I had camped four years before, and I recognized the very spot. The deadwater, a mile or two below it, the Indian called Beskabekukskishtuk, from the lake Beskabekuk, which empties in above. This deadwater, he said, was "a great place for moose always." We saw the grass bent where a moose came out the night before, and the Indian said that he could smell one as far as he could see him; but, he added, that if he should see five or six to-day close by canoe, he no shoot 'em. Accordingly, as he was the only one of the party who had a gun, or had come a-hunting, the moose were safe.

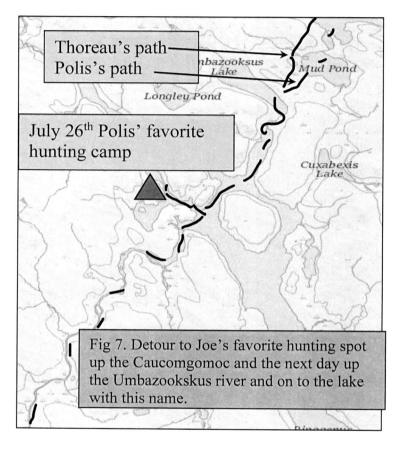

Thoreau's path
Polis's path

July 26th Polis' favorite hunting camp

nbazooksus Lake

Mud Pond

Longley Pond

Cuxabexis Lake

Fig 7. Detour to Joe's favorite hunting spot up the Caucomgomoc and the next day up the Umbazookskus river and on to the lake with this name.

Just below this, a cat owl flew heavily over the stream, and he, asking if I knew what it was, imitated very well the common hoo, hoo, hoo, hoorer, hoo, of our woods; making a hard, guttural sound, "Ugh, ugh, ugh,—ugh, ugh."

When we passed the Moose-horn, he said that it had no name. What Joe Aitteon had called Ragmuff, he called Paytaytequick, and said that it meant Burnt Ground Stream. We stopped there, where I had stopped before, and I bathed in this tributary. It was shallow but cold, apparently too cold for the Indian, who stood looking on. As we were pushing away again, a white-headed eagle sailed over our heads. A reach some miles above Pine Stream, where there were several islands, the Indian said was Nonglangyis Deadwater. Pine Stream he called Black River, and said that its Indian name was Karsaootuk. He could go to Caribou Lake that way.

We carried a part of the baggage about Pine Stream Falls, while the Indian went down in the canoe. A Bangor merchant had told us that two men in his employ were drowned some time ago while passing these falls in a batteau, and a third clung to a rock all night, and was taken off in the morning. There were magnificent great purple fringed orchises on this carry and the neighboring shores. I measured the largest canoe birch which I saw in this journey near the end of the carry. It was 14½ feet in circumference at two feet from the ground, but at five feet divided into three parts. The canoe birches thereabouts were commonly marked by conspicuous dark spiral ridges, with a groove between, so that I thought at first that they had been struck by lightning, but, as the Indian said, it was evidently caused by the grain of the tree. He cut a small, woody knob, as big as a filbert, from the trunk of a fir, apparently an old balsam vesicle filled with wood, which he said was good medicine.

After we had embarked and gone half a mile, my companion remembered that he had left his knife, and we paddled back to get it, against the strong and swift current. This taught us the difference between going up and down the stream, for while we were working our way back a quarter of a mile, we should have gone down a mile and a half at least. So we landed, and while he and the Indian were gone back for it, I watched the motions of the foam, a kind of white water-fowl near the shore, forty or fifty rods below. It alternately appeared and disappeared behind the rock, being carried round by an eddy. Even this semblance of life was interesting on that lonely river.

Immediately below these falls was the Chesuncook Deadwater, caused by the flowing back of the lake. As we paddled slowly over this, the Indian told us a story of his hunting thereabouts, and something more interesting about himself. It appeared that he had represented his tribe at Augusta, and also once at Washington, where he had met some Western chiefs. He had been consulted at Augusta, and gave advice, which he said was followed, respecting the eastern boundary of Maine, as determined by highlands and streams, at the time of the difficulties on that side. He was employed with the surveyors on the line. Also he had called on Daniel Webster in Boston, at the time of his Bunker Hill oration.

I was surprised to hear him say that he liked to go to Boston, New York, Philadelphia, etc., etc.; that he would like to live there. But then, as if relenting a little, when he thought what a poor figure he would make there, he added, "I suppose, I live in New York, I be poorest hunter, I expect." He understood very well both his superiority and his inferiority to the whites. He criticised the people of the United States as compared with other nations, but the only distinct idea with which he labored was, that they were "very strong," but, like some individuals, "too fast." He must have the credit of saying this just before the general breaking down of railroads and banks. He had a great idea of education, and would occasionally break out into such expressions as this, "Kademy—a-cad-e-my—good thing—I suppose they usum Fifth Reader there You been college?"

From this deadwater the outlines of the mountains about Ktaadn were visible. The top

igure 8. Mt. Katadyn view in the center with two peaks.

of Ktaadn was concealed by a cloud, but the Souneunk Mountains were nearer, and quite visible. We steered across the northwest end of the lake, from which we looked down south-southeast, the whole length to Joe Merry Mountain, seen over its extremity. It is an agreeable change to cross a lake, after you have been shut up in the woods, not only on account of the greater expanse of water, but also of sky.

It is one of the surprises which Nature has in store for the traveler in the forest. To look down, in this case, over eighteen miles of water, was liberating and civilizing even. No doubt, the short distance to which you can see in the woods, and the general twilight, would at length react on the inhabitants, and make them salvages. The lakes also reveal the mountains, and give ample scope and range to our thought. The very gulls which we saw sitting on the rocks, like white specks, or circling about, reminded me of custom-house officers. Already there were half a dozen log huts about this end of the lake, though so far from a road. I perceive that in these woods the earliest settlements are, for various reasons, clustering about the lakes, but partly, I think, for the sake of the neighborhood as the oldest clearings. They are forest schools already established,—great centres of light. Water is a pioneer which the settler follows, taking advantage of its improvements.

Thus far only I had been before. About noon we turned northward, up a broad kind of estuary, and at its northeast corner found the Caucomgomoc River, and after going about a mile from the lake, reached the Umbazookskus, which comes in on the right at a point where the former river, coming from the west, turns short to the south. Our course was up the Umbazookskus, but as the Indian knew of a good camping-place, that is, a cool place where there were few mosquitoes about half a mile farther up the Caucomgomoc, we went thither. The latter river, judging from the map, is the longer and principal stream, and, therefore, its name must prevail below the junction. So quickly we changed the civilizing sky of Chesuncook for the dark wood of the Caucomgomoc. On reaching the Indian's camping-ground, on the south side, where the bank was about a dozen feet high, I read on the trunk of a fir tree, blazed by an axe, an inscription in charcoal which had been left by him. It was surmounted by a drawing of a bear paddling a canoe, which he said was the sign which had been used by his family always. The drawing though rude, could not be mistaken for anything but a bear, and he doubted my ability to copy it. The inscription ran thus, verbatim et literatim. I interline the English of his Indian as he gave it to me.

Fig. 9. An evocation of what Joe's mark might have been and his inscription on a tree

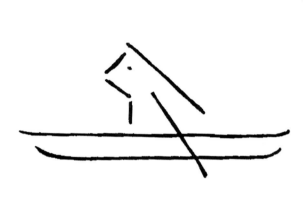

July 26, 1853
Niasoseb.

We alone Joseph,
Polis   elioi
Polis   start
sia   olta
for   Oldtown
onke ni
right away
quambi

July 15, 1855
Niasoseb

This was one of his homes. I saw where he had sometimes stretched his moose-hides on the opposite or sunny north side of the river, where there was a narrow meadow.

He added now below:
1857
July 26,
Io. Polis

After we had selected a place for our camp, and kindled our fire, almost exactly on the site of the Indian's last camp here, he, looking up, observed, "That tree danger." It was a dead part, more than a foot in diameter, of a large canoe birch, which branched at the ground. This branch, rising thirty feet or more, slanted directly over the spot which we had chosen for our bed. I told him to try it with his axe; but he could not shake it perceptibly, and therefore seemed inclined to disregard it, and my companion expressed his willingness to run the risk. But it seemed to me that we should be fools to lie under it, for though the lower part was firm, the top, for aught we knew, might be just ready to fall, and we should at any rate be very uneasy if the wind arose in the night. It is a common accident for men camping in the woods to be killed by a falling tree. So the camp was moved to the other side of the fire.

It was, as usual, a damp and shaggy forest, that Caucomgomoc one, and the most you knew about it was, that on this side it stretched toward the settlements, and on that to still more unfrequented regions. You carried so much topography in your mind always,—and sometimes it seemed to make a considerable difference whether you sat or lay nearer the settlements, or farther off, than your companions,—were the rear or frontier man of the camp. But there is really the same difference between our positions wherever we may be camped, and some are nearer the frontiers on feather-beds in the towns than others on fir twigs in the backwoods.

The Indian said that the Umbazookskus, being a dead stream with broad meadows, was a good place for moose, and he frequently came a-hunting here, being out alone three weeks or more from Oldtown. He sometimes, also, went a-hunting to the Seboois Lakes, taking the stage, with his gun and ammunition, axe and blankets, hard-bread and pork, perhaps for a hundred miles of the way, and jumped off at the wildest place on the road, where he was at once at home, and every rod was a tavern-site for him. Then, after a short journey through the woods, he would build a spruce-bark canoe in one day, putting but few ribs into it, that it might be light, and, after doing his hunting with it on the lakes, would return with his furs the same way he had come. Thus you have an Indian availing himself cunningly of the advantages of civilization, without losing any of his woodcraft, but proving himself the more successful hunter for it.

This man was very clever and quick to learn anything in his line. Our tent was of a kind new to him; but when he had once seen it pitched, it was surprising how quickly he would find and prepare the pole and forked stakes to pitch it with, cutting and placing them right the first time, though I am sure that the majority of white men would have blundered several times.

This river came from Caucomgomoc Lake, about ten miles farther up. Though it was sluggish here, there were falls not far above us, and we saw the foam from them go by from time to time. The Indian said that Caucomgomoc meant Big-Gull Lake (i. e., herring gull, I suppose), gomoc meaning lake. Hence this was Caucomgomoctook, or the river from that lake. This was the Penobscot Caucomgomoctook; there was another St. John one not far north. He finds the eggs of this gull, sometimes twenty together, as big as hen's eggs, on rocky ledges on the west side of Millinocket River, for instance, and eats them.

Now I thought I would observe how he spent his Sunday. While I and my companion were looking about at the trees and river, he went to sleep. Indeed, he improved every opportunity to get a nap, whatever the day. Rambling about the woods at this camp, I noticed that they consisted chiefly of firs, black spruce, and some white, red maple, canoe birch, and, along the river, the hoary alder (*Alnus incana*). I name them in the order of their abundance. The *Viburnum nudum* was a common shrub, and of smaller plants, there were the dwarf cornel, great round-leaved orchis, abundant and in bloom (a greenish-white flower growing in little communities), *Uvularia grandiflora*, whose stem tasted like a cucumber, *Pyrola secunda*, apparently the commonest pyrola in those woods, now out of bloom, *Pyrola elliptica*, and *Chiogenes hispidula*. The Clintonia borealis, with ripe berries, was very abundant, and perfectly at home there. Its leaves, disposed commonly in triangles about its stem, were just as handsomely formed and green, and its berries as blue and glossy, as if it grew by some botanist's favorite path.

I asked the Indian to make us a sugar-bowl of birch bark, which he did, using the great knife which dangled in a sheath from his belt; but the bark broke at the corners when he bent it up, and he said it was not good; that there was a great difference in this respect between the bark of one canoe birch and that of another, i.e., one cracked more easily than another. I used some thin and delicate sheets of this bark which he split and cut, in my flower-book; thinking it would be good to separate the dried specimens from the green.

My companion, wishing to distinguish between the black and white spruce, asked Polis to show him a twig of the latter, which he did at once, together with the black; indeed, he could distinguish them about as far as he could see them; but as the two twigs appeared very much alike, my companion asked the Indian to point out the difference; whereupon the latter, taking the twigs, instantly remarked, as he passed his hand over them successively in a stroking manner, that the white was rough (i.e., the needles stood up nearly perpendicular), but the black smooth (i.e., as if bent or combed down). This was an obvious difference, both to sight and touch. However, if I remember rightly, this would not serve to distinguish the white spruce from the light-colored variety of the black.

I asked him to let me see him get some black spruce root, and make some thread. Whereupon, without looking up at the trees overhead, he began to grub in the ground, instantly distinguishing the black spruce roots, and cutting off a slender one, three or four feet long, and as big as a pipe-stem, he split the end with his knife, and, taking a half between the thumb and forefinger of each hand, rapidly separated its whole length into two equal semicylindrical halves; then giving me another root, he said, "You try." But in my hands it immediately ran off one side, and I got only a very short piece. In short, though it looked very easy, I found that there was a great art in splitting these roots. The split is skillfully humored by bending short with this hand or that, and so kept in the middle. He then took off the bark from each half, pressing a short piece of cedar bark against the convex side with both hands, while he drew the root upward with his teeth. An Indian's teeth are strong, and I noticed that he used his often where we should have used a hand. They amounted to a third hand. He thus obtained, in a moment, a very neat, tough, and flexible string, which he could tie into a knot, or make into a fish-line even. It is said that in Norway and Sweden the roots of the Norway spruce (*Abies excelsa*) are used in the same way for the same purpose. He said that you would be obliged to give half a dollar for spruce root enough for a canoe, thus prepared. He had hired the sewing of his own canoe, though he made all the rest. The root in his canoe was of a pale slate-color, probably acquired by exposure to the weather, or perhaps from being boiled in water first.

He had discovered the day before that his canoe

leaked a little, and said that it was owing to stepping into it violently, which forced the water under the edge of the horizontal seams on the side. I asked him where he would get pitch to mend it with, for they commonly use hard pitch, obtained of the whites at Oldtown. He said that he could make something very similar, and equally good, not of spruce gum, or the like, but of material which we had with us; and he wished me to guess what. But I could not, and he would not tell me, though he showed me a ball of it when made, as big as a pea, and like black pitch, saying, at last, that there were some things which a man did not tell even his wife. It may have been his own discovery. In Arnold's expedition the pioneers used for their canoe "the turpentine of the pine, and the scrapings of the pork-bag."

Being curious to see what kind of fishes there were in this dark, deep, sluggish river, I cast in my line just before night, and caught several small somewhat yellowish sucker-like fishes, which the Indian at once rejected, saying that they were michigan fish (i. e., soft and stinking fish) and good for nothing. Also, he would not touch a pout, which I caught, and said that neither Indians nor whites thereabouts ever ate them, which I thought was singular, since they are esteemed in Massachusetts, and he had told me that he ate hedgehogs, loons, etc. But he said that some small silvery fishes, which I called white chivin, which were similar in size and form to the first, were the best fish in the Penobscot waters, and if I would toss them up the bank to him, he would cook them for me. After cleaning them, not very carefully, leaving the heads on, he laid them on the coals and so broiled them.

Returning from a short walk, he brought a vine in his hand, and asked me if I knew what it was, saying that it made the best tea of anything in the woods. It was the creeping snowberry (*Chiogenes hispidula*), which was quite common there, its berries just grown. He called it cowosnebagosar, which name implies that it grows where old prostrate trunks have collapsed and rotted. So we determined to have some tea made of this tonight. It had a slight checkerberry flavor, and we both agreed that it was really better than the black tea which we had brought. We thought it quite a discovery, and that it might well be dried, and sold in the shops. I, for one, however, am not an old tea-drinker, and cannot speak with authority to others. It would have been particularly good to carry along for a cold drink during the day, the water thereabouts being invariably warm. The Indian said that they also used for tea a certain herb which grew in low ground, which he did not find there, and ledum, or Labrador tea, which I have since found and tried in Concord; also hemlock leaves, the last especially in the winter, when the other plants were covered with snow; and various other things; but he did not approve of arbor-vitæ, which I said I had drunk in those woods. We could have had a new kind of tea every night.

Just before night we saw a musquash (he did not say muskrat), the only one we saw in this voyage, swimming downward on the opposite side of the stream. The Indian, wishing to get one to eat, hushed us, saying, "Stop, me call 'em;" and, sitting flat on the bank, he began to make a curious squeaking, wiry sound with his lips, exerting himself considerably. I was greatly surprised,— thought that I had at last got into the wilderness, and that he was a wild man indeed, to be talking to a musquash! I did not know which of the two was the strangest to me. He seemed suddenly to have quite forsaken humanity, and gone over to the musquash side. The musquash, however, as near as I could see, did not turn aside, though he may have hesitated a little, and the Indian said that he saw our fire; but it was evident that he was in the habit of calling the musquash to him, as he said. An acquaintance of mine who was hunting moose in those woods a month after this, tells me that his Indian in this way repeatedly called the musquash within reach of his paddle in the moonlight, and struck at them. The Indian said a particularly long prayer this Sunday evening, as if to atone for working in the morning.

Comments:

We must add statesman, educator, adviser/consultant and translator to the list of Joe's accomplishments.

This day, a sabbath, is especially rich in dialogue between Thoreau and Polis. They certainly were teaching each other a lot, but were they listening and learning? Perhaps, and being strange opposites, of sorts, not much more should be expected. When Polis observed:

> *'I suppose, I live in New York, I be poorest hunter, I expect.' He understood very well both his superiority and his inferiority to the whites.*

The strangeness of opposites is evident.

The entire dialogue for the day is restful and informative. They had visited one of Joe's favorite hunting camps and looked deeper into Joe's inner self — muskrats, strong lacing cords from spruce roots, herbal teas, reflections on Joe's visits to urban settlements, and so forth. While much of this knowledge is of little interest to those who live in cities, it speaks of another way of life that is in closer harmony with the natural order of the universe-an order that is now imperative to learn about if cities and large populations are to survive at all.

Joe's favorite hunting camp is a maintained camp to this day. But it has a name from decades after Polis: the Canvas Dam. Elements of this dam can still be seen; some canvas is still there. I believe the history of Joe Polis is much more interesting than the lumbermen's use of a dam site for moving logs through. It would be wonderful to have it renamed.

Thoreau included estimates of the length of the Umbazookskus river and the lake of this name. Checking these against current topographical maps shows that he estimated high by a good factor of two.

8. *Vignette 2:* North from South

Joe Polis and Henry Thoreau moved about in the woods by very different means. Their differences are revealed in many dialogues between the two, for example:

> I (*Thoreau*) asked him how he guided himself in the woods. "Oh," said he, "I can tell good many ways." When I (*Thoreau*) pressed him further, he answered, "Sometimes I lookum side-hill," and he glanced toward a high hill or mountain on the eastern shore, "great difference between the north and south, see where the sun has shone most. So trees,—the large limbs bend toward south. Sometimes I lookum locks" (rocks). I asked what he saw on the rocks, but he did not describe anything in particular, answering vaguely, in a mysterious or drawling tone, "Bare locks on lake shore,—great difference between north, south, east, west, side,—can tell what the sun has shone on.

It would not be wise to take Joe's "answering vaguely" as a flaw but rather an indication of a combined rational and inward intuitive sense of knowing as a powerful skill set.

> Suppose, said I (*again, Thoreau*), "that I should take you in a dark night, right up here into the middle of the woods a hundred miles, set you down, and turn

you round quickly twenty times, could you steer straight to Oldtown?" "Oh, yer," said he, "have done pretty much same thing. I will tell you. Some years ago I met an old white hunter at Millinocket; very good hunter. He said he could go anywhere in the woods. He wanted to hunt with me that day, so we start. We chase a moose all the forenoon, round and round, till middle of afternoon, when we kill him. Then I said to him, 'Now you go straight to camp. Don't go round and round where we've been, but go straight.' He said, 'I can't do that, I don't know where I am.' 'Where you think camp?' I asked. He pointed so. Then I laugh at him. I take the lead and go right off the other way, cross our tracks many times, straight camp." "How do you do that?" asked I. "Oh, I can't tell you," he replied. "Great difference between me and white man.

This difference, no doubt, could follow each man's dependence on their degree of using systematic, mental deduction versus an inward, intuitive sense of knowing. When Thoreau and his companion got lost on the carry to Mud Pond:

So I (Thoreau) concluded that on the whole we were on the right course, though as we had come nearly two miles, and saw no signs of Mud Pond, I did harbor the suspicion that we might be on a direct course to Chamberlain Lake, leaving out Mud Pond. This I found by my map would be about five miles northeasterly, and I then took the bearing by my compass.

In most cases, but not all, Joe outwitted Henry with his orienteering except when Henry carefully used his map and compass, which Joe asked to use as well (with Henry). For example, on the 10-mile carry:

> I (Thoreau) had the curiosity to look down carefully, and found that he (Joe) was following his steps backward. I could only occasionally perceive his trail in the moss, and yet he did not appear to look down nor hesitate an instant, but led us out exactly to his canoe. This surprised me; for without a compass, or the sight or noise of the river to guide us, we could not have kept our course many minutes, and could have retraced our steps but a short distance, with a great deal of pains and very slowly, using a laborious circumspection. But it was evident that he could go back through the forest wherever he had been during the day.
>
> The white hunter with whom I talked in the stage knew some of the resources of the Indian. He said that he steered by the wind, or by the limbs of the hemlocks, which were largest on the south side; also sometimes, when he knew that there was a lake near, by firing his gun and listening to hear the direction and distance of the echo from over it.

9. July 27- Umbazookskus, Mud Pond, Apmoojenegamook

After a long while my companion came back, and the Indian with him. We had taken the wrong road…

Having rapidly loaded the canoe, which the Indian always carefully attended to, that it might be well trimmed, and each having taken a look, as usual, to see that nothing was left, we set out again descending the Caucomgomoc, and turning northeasterly up the Umbazookskus. This name, the Indian said, meant Much Meadow River. We found it a very meadowy stream, and deadwater, and now very wide on account of the rains, though, he said, it was sometimes quite narrow. The space between the woods, chiefly bare meadow, was from fifty to two hundred rods in breadth, and is a rare place for moose. It reminded me of the Concord; and what increased the resemblance was one old musquash-house almost afloat.

It was unusual for the woods to be so distant from the shore, and there was quite an echo from them, but when I was shouting in order to awake it, the Indian reminded me that I should scare the moose, which he was looking out for, and which we all wanted to see. The word for echo was

Pockadunkquaywayle.

While we were thus employed, two Indians in a canoe hove in sight round the bushes, coming down stream. Our Indian knew one of them, an old man, and fell into conversation with him in Indian. He belonged at the foot of Moosehead. The other was of another tribe. They were returning from hunting. I asked the younger if they had seen any moose, to which he said no; but I, seeing the moose-hides sticking out from a great bundle made with their blankets in the middle of the canoe, added, "Only their hides." As he was a foreigner, he may have wished to deceive me, for it is against the law for white men and foreigners to kill moose in Maine at this season. But perhaps he need not have been alarmed, for the moose-wardens are not very particular. I heard quite directly of one who being asked by a white man going into the woods what he would say if he killed a moose, answered, "If you bring me a quarter of it, I guess you won't be troubled." His duty being, as he said, only to prevent the "indiscriminate" slaughter of them for their hides. I suppose that he would consider it an indiscriminate slaughter when a quarter was not reserved for himself. Such are the perquisites of this office.

We saw some fresh moose-tracks along the shore, but the Indian said that the moose were not driven out of the woods by the flies, as usual at this season, on account of the abundance of water everywhere. The stream was only from one and one half to three rods wide, quite winding, with occasional small islands, meadows, and some very swift and shallow places. When we came to an island, the Indian never hesitated which side to take, as if the current told him which was the shortest and deepest. It was lucky for us that the water was so high. We had to walk but once on this stream, carrying a part of the load, at a swift and shallow reach, while he got up with the canoe, not being obliged to take out, though he said it was very strong water. Once or twice we passed the red wreck of a batteau which had been stove some spring.

While making this portage I saw many splendid specimens of the great purple fringed orchis, three feet high. It is remarkable that such delicate flowers should here adorn these wilderness paths.

Having resumed our seats in the canoe, I felt the Indian wiping my back, which he had accidentally spat upon. He said it was a sign that I was going to be married.

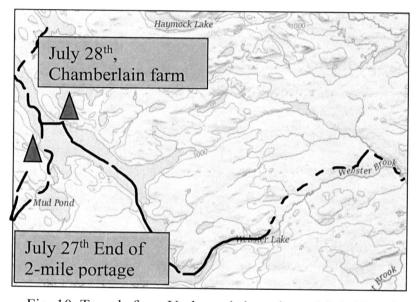

Fig. 10. Travels from Umbazookskus, through Mud Pond (Joe only), through the swamps lost (Henry and companion), and then into various parts of Chamberlain Lake continuing on to the 10 mile portage and then on to Lake Matagamon.

The Umbazookskus River is called ten miles long. Having poled up the narrowest part some three or four miles, the next opening in the sky was over Umbazookskus Lake, which we suddenly entered about eleven o'clock in the forenoon. It stretches northwesterly four or five miles, with what the Indian called the Caucomgomoc Mountain seen far beyond it. It was an agreeable change.

Mud Pond is about halfway from Umbazookskus to Chamberlain Lake, into which it empties, and to which we were bound. The Indian said that this was the wettest carry in the State, and as the season was a very wet one, we anticipated an unpleasant walk. As usual he made one large bundle of the pork-keg, cooking-utensils, and other loose traps, by tying them up in his blanket. We should be obliged to go over the carry twice, and our method was to carry one half part way, and then go back for the rest.

Our path ran close by the door of a log hut in a clearing at this end of the carry, which the Indian, who alone entered it, found to be occupied by a Canadian and his family, and that the man had been blind for a year. He seemed peculiarly unfortunate to be taken blind there, where there were so few eyes to see for him. He could not even be led out of that country by a dog, but must be taken down the rapids as passively as a barrel of flour. This was the first house above Chesuncook, and the last on the

Penobscot waters, and was built here, no doubt, because it was the route of the lumberers in the winter and spring.

After a slight ascent from the lake through the springy soil of the Canadian's clearing, we entered on a level and very wet and rocky path through the universal dense evergreen forest, a loosely paved gutter merely, where we went leaping from rock to rock and from side to side, in the vain attempt to keep out of the water and mud. We concluded that it was yet Penobscot water, though there was no flow to it. It was on this carry that the white hunter whom I met in the stage, as he told me, had shot two bears a few months before. They stood directly in the path, and did not turn out for him. They might be excused for not turning out there, or only taking the right as the law directs. He said that at this season bears were found on the mountains and hillsides in search of berries, and were apt to be saucy,—that we might come across them up Trout Stream; and he added, what I hardly credited, that many Indians slept in their canoes, not daring to sleep on land, on account of them.

Here commences what was called, twenty years ago, the best timber land in the State. This very spot was described as "covered with the greatest abundance of pine," but now this appeared to me, comparatively, an uncommon tree there,— and yet you did not see where any more could have stood, amid the dense growth of cedar, fir, etc. It was then proposed to cut a canal from lake to lake here, but the outlet was finally made farther east, at Telos Lake, as we shall see.

The Indian with his canoe soon disappeared before us; but ere long he came back and told us to take a path which turned off westward, it being better walking, and, at my suggestion, he agreed to leave a bough in the regular carry at that place, that we might not pass it by mistake. Thereafter, he said, we were to keep the main path, and he added, "You see 'em my tracks." But I had not much faith that we could distinguish his tracks, since others had passed over the carry within a few days.

We turned off at the right place, but were soon confused by numerous logging- paths, coming into the one we were on, by which lumberers had been to pick out those pines which I have mentioned. However, we kept what we considered the main path, though it was a winding one, and in this, at long intervals, we distinguished a faint trace of a footstep. This, though comparatively unworn, was at first a better, or, at least, a drier road than the regular carry which we had left. It led through an arbor-vitæ wilderness of the grimmest character. The great fallen and rotting trees had been cut through and rolled aside, and their huge trunks abutted on the path on each side, while others still lay across it two or three feet high. It was impossible for us to discern the Indian's trail in the elastic moss, which, like a thick carpet, covered every rock and fallen tree, as well as the earth. Nevertheless, I did occasionally detect the track of a man, and I gave myself some credit for it. I carried my whole load at once, a heavy knapsack, and a large india-rubber bag, containing our bread and a blanket, swung on a paddle; in all, about sixty pounds; but my companion preferred to make two journeys, by short stages, while I waited for him. We could not be sure that we were not depositing our loads each time farther off from the true path.

After I had sat there some time, I noticed at this fork in the path a tree which had been blazed, and the letters "Chamb. L." written on it with red chalk. This I knew to mean Chamberlain Lake. So I concluded that on the whole we were on the right course, though as we had come nearly two miles, and saw no signs of Mud Pond, I did harbor the suspicion that we might be on a direct course to Chamberlain Lake, leaving out Mud Pond. This I found by my map would be about five miles northeasterly, and I then took the bearing by my compass.

My companion having returned with his bag, and also defended his face and hands with the insect-wash, we set forward again. The walking rapidly grew worse, and the path more indistinct, and at length, after passing through a patch of *Calla palustris*, still abundantly in bloom, we found ourselves in a more open and regular swamp, made less passable than ordinary by the unusual wetness of the season. We sank a foot deep in water and mud at every step, and sometimes up to our knees, and the trail was almost obliterated, being no more than that a musquash leaves in similar places, when he parts the floating sedge. In fact, it probably was a musquash trail in some places. We concluded that if Mud Pond was as muddy as the approach to it was wet, it certainly deserved its name. It would have been amusing to behold the dogged and deliberate pace at which we entered that swamp, without interchanging a word, as if determined to go through it, though it should come up to our necks. Having penetrated a considerable distance into this, and found a tussock on which we could deposit our loads, though there was no place to sit, my companion went back for the rest of his pack. I had thought to observe on this carry when we crossed the dividing line between the Penobscot and St. John, but as my feet had hardly been out of water the whole distance, and it was all level and stagnant, I began to despair of finding it. I remembered hearing a good deal about the "highlands" dividing the waters of the Penobscot from those of the St. John, as well as the St. Lawrence, at the time of the northeast boundary dispute, and I observed by my map, that the line claimed by Great Britain as the boundary prior to 1842 passed between Umbazookskus Lake and Mud Pond, so that we had either crossed or were then on it. These, then, according to her interpretation of the treaty of '83, were the "highlands which divide those rivers that empty themselves into the St. Lawrence from those which fall into the Atlantic Ocean." Truly an interesting spot to stand on,— if that were it,—though you could not sit down there. I thought that if the commissioners themselves, and the King of Holland with them, had spent a few days here, with their packs upon their backs, looking for that "highland," they would have had an interesting time, and perhaps it would have modified their views of the question somewhat. The King of Holland would have been in his element. Such were my meditations while my companion was gone back for his bag.

After a long while my companion came back, and the Indian with him. We had taken the wrong road, and the Indian had lost us. He had very wisely gone back to the Canadian's camp, and asked him which way we had probably gone, since he could better understand the ways of white men, and he told him correctly that we had undoubtedly taken the supply road to Chamberlain Lake (slender supplies they would get over such a road at this season). The Indian was greatly surprised that we should have taken what he called a "tow" (i. e., tote or toting or supply) road, instead of a carry path,—that we had not followed his tracks,—said it was "strange," and evidently thought little of our woodcraft.

Having held a consultation, and eaten a mouthful of bread, we concluded that it would perhaps be nearer for us two now to keep on to Chamberlain Lake, omitting Mud Pond, than to go back and start anew for the last place, though the Indian had never been through this way, and knew nothing about it. In the meanwhile he would go back and finish carrying over his canoe and bundle to Mud Pond, cross that, and go down its outlet and up Chamberlain Lake, and trust to meet us there before night. It was now a little after noon. He supposed that the water in which we stood had flowed back from Mud Pond, which could not be far off eastward, but was unapproachable through the dense cedar swamp.

Having gone about a mile, and got into low ground again, I heard a noise like the note of an owl, which I soon discovered to be made by the Indian, and, answering him, we soon came together. He had reached the lake, after crossing Mud Pond, and running some rapids below it, and had come up about a mile and a half on our path. If he had not come back to meet us, we probably should not have found him that night, for the path branched once or twice before reaching this particular part of the lake. So he went back for my companion and his bag, while I kept on. Having waded through another stream, where the bridge of logs had been broken up and half floated away,— and this was not altogether worse than our ordinary walking, since it was less muddy,—we continued on, through alternate mud and water, to the shore of Apmoojenegamook Lake, which we reached in season for a late supper, instead of dining there, as we had expected, having gone without our dinner. It was at least five miles by the way we had come, and as my companion had gone over most of it three times, he had walked full a dozen miles, bad as it was. In the winter, when the water is frozen, and the snow is four feet deep, it is no doubt a tolerable path to a footman. As it was, I would not have missed that walk for a good deal. If you want an exact recipe for making such a road, take one part Mud Pond, and dilute it with equal parts of Umbazookskus and Apmoojenegamook; then send a family of musquash through to locate it, look after the grades and culverts, and finish it to their minds, and let a hurricane follow to do the fencing.

We had come out on a point extending into Apmoojenegamook, or Chamberlain Lake, west of the outlet of Mud Pond, where there was a broad, gravelly, and rocky shore, encumbered with bleached logs and trees. We were rejoiced to see such dry things in that part of the world. But at first we did not attend to dryness so much as to mud and wetness. We all three walked into the lake up to our middle to wash our clothes.

This was another noble lake, called twelve miles long, east and west; if you add Telos Lake, which, since the dam was built, has been connected with it by dead water, it will be twenty; and it is apparently from a mile and a half to two miles wide. We were about midway its length, on the south side. We could see the only clearing in these parts, called the "Chamberlain Farm," with two or three log buildings close together, on the opposite shore, some two and a half miles distant. The smoke of our fire on the shore brought over two men in a canoe from the farm, that being a common signal agreed on when one wishes to cross. It took them about half an hour to come over, and they had their labor for their pains this time. Even the English name of the lake had a wild, woodland sound, reminding me of that Chamberlain who killed Paugus at Lovewell's fight.

After putting on such dry clothes as we had, and hanging the others to dry on the pole which the Indian arranged over the fire, we ate our supper, and lay down on the pebbly shore with our feet to the fire, without pitching our tent, making a thin bed of grass to cover the stones.

Here first I was molested by the little midge called the no-see-em *(Simulium nocivum,*—the latter word is not the Latin for no-see-em), especially over the sand at the water's edge, for it is a kind of sand-fly. You would not observe them but for their light-colored wings. They are said to get under your clothes, and produce a feverish heat, which I suppose was what I felt that night.

Our insect foes in this excursion, to sum them up, were, first, mosquitoes, the chief ones, but only troublesome at night, or when we sat still on shore by day; second, black flies (*Simulium molestum*), which molested us more or less on the carries by day, as I have before described, and sometimes in narrower parts of the stream. Harris mistakes when he says that they are not seen after June. Third, moose-flies. The big ones, Polis said, were called Bososquasis. It is a stout, brown fly, much like a horse-fly, about eleven sixteenths of an inch long, commonly rusty-colored beneath, with unspotted wings. They can bite smartly, according to Polis, but are easily avoided or killed. Fourth, the no-see-ems above mentioned. Of all these, the mosquitoes are the only ones that troubled me seriously; but, as I was provided with a wash and a veil, they have not made any deep impression.

The Indian would not use our wash to protect his face and hands, for fear that it would hurt his skin, nor had he any veil; he, therefore, suffered from insects now, and throughout this journey, more than either of us. I think that he suffered more than I did, when neither of us was protected. He regularly tied up his face in his handkerchief, and buried it in his blanket, and he now finally lay down on the sand between us and the fire for the sake of the smoke, which he tried to make enter his blanket about his face, and for the same purpose he lit his pipe and breathed the smoke into his blanket.

As we lay thus on the shore, with nothing between us and the stars, I inquired what stars he was acquainted with, or had names for. They were the Great Bear, which he called by this name, the Seven Stars, which he had no English name for, "the morning star," and "the north star."

I was awakened at midnight by some heavy, low-flying bird, probably a loon, flapping by close over my head, along the shore. So, turning the other side of my half-clad body to the fire, I sought slumber again.

Comments:

As portages can be, this one was pure misery. Thoreau reached the height of dark humor when he said:

> *If you want an exact recipe for making such a road, take one part Mud Pond, and dilute it with equal parts of Umbazookskus and Apmoojenegamook; then send a family of musquash through to locate it, look after the grades and culverts, and finish it to their minds, and let a hurricane follow to do the fencing.*

The entire trip had various short carries or portages, but only two major ones: the present one from Umbazookus to Mud pond to Chamberlain and a later 10 mile portage from Webster Lake to The East Branch of the Penobscot or Grand Lake Matagamon (not counting the first 2 mile carry along a road from Moosehead Lake to the West Branch of the Penobscot).

Henry and his companion got badly lost and in some peril on the 2 mile and the 10 mile portages. This fact raises several deep questions about navigation skills, communication skills and leadership. The same issues play out every week in modern life as people enter into various wilderness adventures and make mistakes. Most readers are aware of the dictum: if lost, stay put and others will (should) find you. If a guide is involved, his/her duty is to find the lost ones and bring them to safety. Did not Joe do just that? What communication, navigation and leadership skills worked to this end and what weaknesses are found in this real account? If these questions seem melodramatic, Henry David later grieves that he may never see his companion again and how would he ever break this to the man's kin?

As noted above:

> After I had sat there some time, I noticed at this fork in the path a tree which had been blazed, and the letters Chamb. L. written on it with red chalk. This I knew to mean Chamberlain Lake. So I concluded that on the whole we were on the right course, though as we had come nearly two miles, and saw no signs of Mud Pond, I did harbor the suspicion that we might be on a direct course to Chamberlain Lake, leaving out Mud Pond. This I found by my map would be about five miles northeasterly, and I then took the bearing by my compass.

This is a very nice use of map and compass but far too late. They should have been used at the blind man's cabin to get a good heading for their travels and to discuss their plan with Joe and *perhaps within earshot of the blind man who probably could have added information. Knowing the correct heading and checking the compass frequently would, for an experienced woodsman, have informed them well at each junction on their trek.*

But it is easy to misuse a compass and this fact does not arise in Thoreau's commentaries. The easiest example is to use a compass underwater while scuba diving. One can set a compass direction and follow it carefully only to miss the target wide of the mark if there is any side current (there often is) to push one off the mark. The same is true in a forest even without any effective side current as following any compass bearing is most likely to encounter many trees, rocks and so forth in one's way. In each case one must select a nearby object that falls on the line of travel, proceed to it, and then choose another reference point up ahead, hence 'leap frogging' from one marker to another. Still Thoreau is to be complimented for making good usage of map and compass for his trip.

10. July 28- Rain

…and he lamented that the present generation of Indians "had lost a great deal."

When we awoke, we found a heavy dew on our blankets. I lay awake very early, and listened to the clear, shrill ah, *te te, te te, te* of the white-throated sparrow, repeated at short intervals, without the least variation, for half an hour, as if it could not enough express its happiness. Whether my companions heard it or not, I know not, but it was a kind of matins to me, and the event of that forenoon. It was a pleasant sunrise, and we had a view of the mountains in the southeast. Ktaadn appeared about southeast by south. A double-topped mountain, about southeast by east, and another portion of the same, east-southeast. The last the Indian called Nerlumskeechticook, and said that it was at the head of the East Branch, and we should pass near it on our return that way.

We did some more washing in the lake this morning, and with our clothes hung about on the dead trees and rocks, the shore looked like washing-day at home. The Indian, taking the hint, borrowed the soap, and, walking into the lake, washed his only cotton shirt on his person, then put on his pants and let it dry on him.

I observed that he wore a cotton shirt, originally white, a greenish flannel one over it, but no waistcoat, flannel drawers, and strong linen or duck pants, which also had been white, blue woolen stockings, cowhide boots, and a Kossuth hat. He carried no change of clothing, but putting on a stout, thick jacket, which he laid aside in the canoe, and seizing a full-sized axe, his gun and ammunition, and a blanket, which would do for a sail or knapsack, if wanted, and strapping on his belt, which contained a large sheath-knife, he walked off at once, ready to be gone all summer. This looked very independent; a few simple and effective tools, and no india-rubber clothing. He was always the first ready to start in the morning, and if it had not held some of our property, would not have been obliged to roll up his blanket. Instead of carrying a large bundle of his own extra clothing, etc., he brought back the greatcoats of moose tied up in his blanket. I found that his outfit was the result of a long experience, and in the main hardly to be improved on, unless by washing and an extra shirt. Wanting a button here, he walked off to a place where some Indians had recently encamped, and searched for one, but I believe in vain.

Having softened our stiffened boots and shoes with the pork fat, the usual disposition of what was left at breakfast, we crossed the lake early, steering in a diagonal direction, northeasterly about four miles, to the outlet, which was not to be discovered till we were close to it. The Indian name, Apmoojenegamook, means lake that is crossed, because the usual course lies across, and not along it. This is the largest of the Allegash lakes, and was the first St. John water that we floated on. It is shaped in the main like Chesuncook. There are no mountains or high hills very near it. At Bangor we had been told of a township many miles farther northwest; it was indicated to us as containing the highest land thereabouts, where, by climbing a particular tree in the forest, we could get a general idea of the country. I have no doubt that the last was good advice, but we did not go there. We did not intend to go far down the Allegash, but merely to get a view of the great lakes which are its source, and then return this way to the East Branch of the Penobscot. The water now, by good rights, flowed northward, if it could be said to flow at all.

After reaching the middle of the lake, we found the waves as usual pretty high, and the Indian warned my companion, who was nodding, that he must not allow himself to fall asleep in the canoe lest he should upset us; adding, that when Indians want to sleep in a canoe, they lie down straight on the bottom. But in this crowded one that was impossible. However, he said that he would nudge him if he saw him nodding.

We were now fairly on the Allegash River, which name our Indian said meant hemlock bark. These waters flow northward about one hundred miles, at first very feebly, then southeasterly two hundred and fifty more to the Bay of Fundy. After perhaps two miles of river, we entered Heron Lake, called on the map Pongokwahem, scaring up forty or fifty young shecorways, sheldrakes, at the entrance, which ran over the water with great rapidity, as usual in a long line.

This was the fourth great lake, lying northwest and southeast, like Chesuncook and most of the long lakes in that neighborhood, and, judging from the map, it is about ten miles long. We had entered it on the southwest side, and saw a dark mountain northeast over the lake, not very far off nor high, which the Indian said was called Peaked Mountain, and used by explorers to look for timber from. There was also some other high land more easterly. The shores were in the same ragged and unsightly condition, encumbered with dead timber, both fallen and standing, as in the last lake, owing to the dam on the Allegash below. Some low points or islands were almost drowned.

I saw something white a mile off on the water, which turned out to be a great gull on a rock in the middle, which the Indian would have been glad to kill and eat, but it flew away long before we were near; and also a flock of summer ducks that were about the rock with it. I asked him about herons, since this was Heron Lake, he said that he found the blue heron's nests in the hardwood trees. I thought that I saw a light-colored object move along the opposite or northern shore, four or five miles distant. He did not know what it could be, unless it were a moose, though he had never seen a white one; but he said that he could distinguish a moose "anywhere on shore, clear across the lake."

We landed on the southeast side of the island, which was rather elevated and densely wooded, with a rocky shore, in season for an early dinner. Somebody had camped there not long before, and left the frame on which they stretched a moose-hide, which our Indian criticised severely, thinking it showed but little woodcraft. Here were plenty of the shells of crayfish, or fresh-water lobsters, which had been washed ashore, such as have given a name to some ponds and streams. They are commonly four or five inches long. The Indian proceeded at once to cut a canoe birch, slanted it up against another tree on the shore, tying it with a withe, and lay down to sleep in its shade.

When we were on the Caucomgomoc, he recommended to us a new way home, the very one which we had first thought of, by the St. John. He even said that it was easier, and would take but little more time than the other, by the East Branch of the Penobscot, though very much farther round; and taking the map, he showed where we should be each night, for he was familiar with the route. According to his calculation, we should reach the French settlements the next night after this, by keeping northward down the Allegash, and when we got into the main St. John the banks would be more or less settled all the way; as if that were a recommendation. There would be but one or two falls, with short carrying-places, and we should go down the stream very fast, even a hundred miles a day, if the wind allowed; and he indicated where we should carry over into Eel River to save a bend below Woodstock in New Brunswick, and so into the Schoodic Lake, and thence to the Mattawamkeag. It would be about three hundred and sixty miles to Bangor this way, though only about one hundred and sixty by the other; but in the former case we should explore the St. John from its source through two thirds of its course, as well as the Schoodic Lake and Mattawamkeag,—and we were again tempted to go that way. I feared, however, that the banks of the St. John were too much settled. When I asked him which course would take us through the wildest country, he said the route by the East Branch. Partly from this consideration, as also from its shortness, we resolved to adhere to the latter route, and perhaps ascend Ktaadn on the way. We made this island the limit of our excursion in this direction.

Polis had evidently more curiosity respecting the few settlers in those woods than we. If nothing was said, he took it for granted that we wanted to go straight to the next log-hut. Having observed that we came by the log huts at Chesuncook, and the blind Canadian's at the Mud Pond carry, without stopping to communicate with the inhabitants, he took occasion now to suggest that the usual way was, when you came near a house, to go to it, and tell the inhabitants what you had seen or heard, and then they tell you what they had seen; but we laughed, and said that we had had enough of houses for the present, and had come here partly to avoid them.

In the meanwhile, the wind, increasing, blew down the Indian's birch, and created such a sea that we found ourselves prisoners on the island, the nearest shore, which was the western, being perhaps a mile distant, and we took the canoe out to prevent its drifting away. We did not know but we should be compelled to spend the rest of the day and the night there. At any rate, the Indian went to sleep again in the shade of his birch, my companion busied himself drying his plants, and I rambled along the shore westward, which was quite stony, and obstructed with fallen, bleached, or drifted trees for four or five rods in width.

Our Indian said that he was a doctor, and could tell me some medicinal use for every plant I could show him. I immediately tried him. He said that the inner bark of the aspen (*Populus tremuloides*) was good for sore eyes; and so with various other plants, proving himself as good as his word. According to his account, he had acquired such knowledge in his youth from a wise old Indian with whom he associated, and he lamented that the present generation of Indians "had lost a great deal."

He said that the caribou was a "very great runner," that there was none about this lake now, though there used to be many, and pointing to the belt of dead trees caused by the dams, he added, "No likum stump,—when he sees that he scared."

Pointing southeasterly over the lake and distant forest, he observed, "Me go Oldtown in three days." I asked how he would get over the swamps and fallen trees. "Oh," said he, "in winter all covered, go anywhere on snowshoes, right across lakes." When I asked how he went, he said, "First I go Ktaadn, west side, then I go Millinocket, then Pamadumcook, then Nicketow, then Lincoln, then Oldtown," or else he went a shorter way by the Piscataquis. What a wilderness walk for a man to take alone! None of your half-mile swamps, none of your mile-wide woods merely, as on the skirts of our towns, without hotels, only a dark mountain or a lake for guide-board and station, over ground much of it impassable in summer!

It reminded me of *Prometheus Bound*. Here was traveling of the old heroic kind over the unaltered face of nature. From the Allegash, or Hemlock River, and Pongoquahem Lake, across great Apmoojenegamook, and leaving the Nerlumskeechticook Mountain on his left, he takes his way under the bear- haunted slopes of Souneunk and Ktaadn Mountains to Pamadumcook, and Millinocket's inland seas (where often gulls'-eggs may increase his store), and so on to the forks of the Nicketow (niasoseb, "we alone Joseph," seeing what our folks see), ever pushing the boughs of the fir and spruce aside, with his load of furs, contending day and night, night and day, with the shaggy demon vegetation, traveling through the mossy graveyard of trees. Or he could go by "that rough tooth of the sea," Kineo, great source of arrows and of spears to the ancients, when weapons of stone were used. Seeing and hearing moose, caribou, bears, porcupines, lynxes, wolves, and panthers. Places where he might live and die and never hear of the United States, which make such a noise in the world,—never hear of America, so called from the name of a European gentleman.

As we lay huddled together under the tent,

which leaked considerably about the sides, with our baggage at our feet, we listened to some of the grandest thunder which I ever heard,—rapid peals, round and plump, bang, bang, bang, in succession, like artillery from some fortress in the sky; and the lightning was proportionally brilliant. The Indian said, "It must be good powder." All for the benefit of the moose and us, echoing far over the concealed lakes. I thought it must be a place which the thunder loved, where the lightning practiced to keep its hand in, and it would do no harm to shatter a few pines. What had become of the *ephemeræ* and devil's-needles then? Were they prudent enough to seek harbor before the storm? Perhaps their motions might guide the voyageur.

Looking out I perceived that the violent shower falling on the lake had almost instantaneously flattened the waves,—the commander of that fortress had smoothed it for us so,—and, it clearing off, we resolved to start immediately, before the wind raised them again.

Going outside, I said that I saw clouds still in the southwest, and heard thunder there. The Indian asked if the thunder went "lound" (round), saying that if it did we should have more rain. I thought that it did. We embarked, nevertheless, and paddled rapidly back toward the dams. The white-throated sparrows on the shore were about, singing, *Ah, te-e-e, te-e-e, te,* or else *ah, te- e-e, te-e-e, te-e-e, te-e-e.*

At the outlet of Chamberlain Lake we were overtaken by another gusty rain- storm, which compelled us to take shelter, the Indian under his canoe on the bank, and we ran under the edge of the dam. However, we were more scared than wet. From my covert I could see the Indian peeping out from beneath his canoe to see what had become of the rain. When we had taken our respective places thus once or twice, the rain not coming down in earnest, we commenced rambling about the neighborhood, for the wind had by this time raised such waves on the lake that we could not stir, and we feared that we should be obliged to camp there. We got an early supper on the dam and tried for fish there, while waiting for the tumult to subside. The fishes were not only few, but small and worthless, and the Indian declared that there were no good fishes in the St. John's waters; that we must wait till we got to the Penobscot waters.

We could not have landed if we would, without the greatest danger of being swamped; so blow as it might, we must depend on coasting by it. It was twilight, too, and that stormy cloud was advancing rapidly in our rear. It was a pleasant excitement, yet we were glad to reach, at length, in the dusk, the cleared shore of the Chamberlain Farm.

We landed on a low and thinly wooded point there, and while my companions were pitching the tent, I ran up to the house to get some sugar, our six pounds being gone;—it was no wonder they were, for Polis had a sweet tooth. He would first fill his dipper nearly a third full of sugar, and then add the coffee to it. Here was a clearing extending back from the lake to a hilltop, with some dark-colored log buildings and a storehouse in it, and half a dozen men standing in front of the principal hut, greedy for news. Among them was the man who tended the dam on the Allegash and tossed the bullet. He having charge of the dams, and learning that we were going to Webster Stream the next day, told me that some of their men, who were haying at Telos Lake, had shut the dam at the canal there in order to catch trout, and if we wanted more water to take us through the canal, we might raise the gate, for he would like to have it raised. The Chamberlain woods Farm is no doubt a cheerful opening in the woods, but such was the lateness of the hour that it has left but a dusky impression on my mind. As I have said, the influx of light merely is civilizing, yet I fancied that they walked about on Sundays in their clearing somewhat as in a prison-yard.

They were unwilling to spare more than four pounds of brown sugar,— unlocking the storehouse to get it,—since they only kept a little for such cases as this, and they charged twenty cents a pound for it, which certainly it was worth to get it up there.

When I returned to the shore it was quite dark, but we had a rousing fire to warm and dry us by, and a snug apartment behind it. The Indian went up to the house to inquire after a brother who had been absent hunting a year or two, and while another shower was beginning, I groped about cutting spruce and arbor-vitæ twigs for a bed. I preferred the arbor-vitæ on account of its fragrance, and spread it particularly thick about the shoulders. It is remarkable with what pure satisfaction the traveler in these woods will reach his camping-ground on the eve of a tempestuous night like this, as if he had got to his inn, and, rolling himself in his blanket, stretch himself on his six-feet-by-two bed of dripping fir twigs, with a thin sheet of cotton for roof, snug as a meadow-mouse in its nest. Invariably our best nights were those when it rained, for then we were not troubled with mosquitoes.

You soon come to disregard rain on such excursions, at least in the summer, it is so easy to dry yourself, supposing a dry change of clothing is not to be had. You can much sooner dry you by such a fire as you can make in the woods than in anybody's kitchen, the fireplace is so much larger, and wood so much more abundant. A shed-shaped tent will catch and reflect the heat like a Yankee baker, and you may be drying while you are sleeping.

Some who have leaky roofs in the towns may have been kept awake, but we were soon lulled asleep by a steady, soaking rain, which lasted all night. To- night, the rain not coming at once with violence, the twigs were soon dried by the reflected heat.

Comments:

> *...he had acquired such knowledge in his youth from a wise old Indian with whom he associated, and he lamented that the present generation of Indians 'had lost a great deal.'*

Indeed, Thoreau was very fortunate to happen upon Joe Polis to be his guide, as the next day would show.

Polis' gave the Indian name for Chamberlain Lake, Apmoojenegamook, which is instructive. He explains that it is the lake that must be crossed which might be misunderstood. Many of the lakes in northern Maine work well when paddled length wise as they can make a good circuit but this lake doesn't conform and may have to be crossed in the middle to proceed northerly. Winds will develop along the length of the lake quite easily to the detriment of those who need to cross in a rather wide part of the lake, which can be hazardous. The name itself calls for caution.

On the 28th, Thoreau confirmed that his greatest purpose for this trip was to deeply explore "wilderness" in the Northeast part of the United States. After Joe Polis proposed an alternate route going North by the St. Croix river, Thoreau asked Polis which route was the wildest, to which Joe replied, "...by the east branch...". This confirms the goal set out by Thoreau at the beginning of his recorded trip. By contrast, Polis had set the goal of getting some Moose hide and making money.

11. *Vignette 3,* Design of a Tent

Some of the apparatus of camping, circa 1857, is well described in Thoreau's writing and gives the reader an opportunity to see just how things have changed until now. We shall study a few of these changes in several vignettes.

Concerning tents, Thoreau's tent is remarkably similar to the tent that I used from the time I was about 11 years old until I was about 16. I have progressed through about nine different tents, and I have marveled at the technology and the design evolution over the years.

Understanding Thoreau's tent is perhaps a bit tricky. Let's look at several statements, taken from his text and sort out this puzzle.

> Our tent was of thin cotton cloth and quite small, forming with the ground a triangular prism closed at the rear end, six feet long, seven wide, and four high, so that we could barely sit up in the middle. It required two forked stakes, a smooth ridge-pole, and a dozen or more pins to pitch it.

This tent was a so-called 'tarp tent,' a name used while I was growing up. It can be pitched in multiple ways according to ones' needs. It appears that they may have adapted to such needs and may have used at least two modalities on this trip. The phrase "…forming with the ground a triangular prism…," and using a ridge pole, and they could barely sit up in the middle (presumably the highest point in the tent) leads one to believe that it resembled a classic pup tent or any similar central ridge pole tent, as are still rather common today. The large number of stakes (pins) suggest that it was fastened by the stakes on each side of the tent firmly to the ground and should resist strong winds. But how they closed it at one end is unclear, and readers must make a guess for themselves.

The second modality is a modification of the first:

> A shed-shaped tent will catch and reflect the heat like a Yankee baker, and you may be drying while you are sleeping.

Another similar more modern name was a "Baker" tent, and he uses this term when comparing to a Yankee baker, which I presume is a reflector oven that has been popular for many decades and perhaps centuries. The tent of the first description is very difficult to heat but this second one is easy, and they commonly put a VERY LARGE fire in front of the tent for warmth, to dry their clothes and perhaps to drive off some of the mosquitoes.

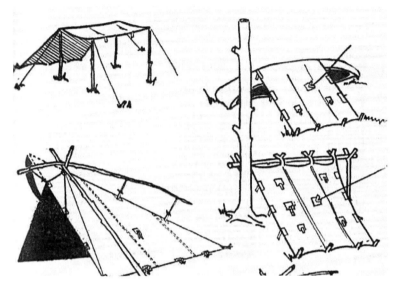

Figure 11. Four variants of the pitched 'Tarp" tent. I have used three of them on various canoe and kayak trips in the 1950's and 60's. Thoreau's group used several also with their 'sheet' tent. From the author's June 1954 copy of the Handbook for Boys, copyright 1948.

There are many other ways to pitch a tarp tent and Fig. 11 shows some of them. But how dry could you sleep within these tents?

> …with a thin sheet of cotton for roof, snug as a meadow-mouse in its nest. Invariably our best nights were those when it rained, for then we were not troubled with mosquitoes…

> It kept off dew and wind, and an ordinary (emphasis added) rain, and answered our purpose well enough.

Elsewhere, Thoreau mentions that in a strong storm there would be a fine spray of water falling on them from this 'thin sheet of cotton,' so his tent was not fully dry. All the tents that I used before I was twenty years old were made of canvas, which had to be chemically treated to reduce or nearly eliminate any water seeping through but not so with Thoreau's tent. Canvas is traditionally made of either linen or cotton with some other fibers occasionally added. So, the tents of my youth and Thoreau's tent were quite similar except that canvas is thicker and heavier and ours were treated. But the same leakage problem could exist if the treatment was not renewed regularly or if a tent mate would rub his finger on the inside of the tent right over your head causing canvas to leak, usually ending in a fist fight with the perpetrator having to sleep under the leak.

Today's tents are a marvel of technology. They contain their own poles and pegs, so we do not need to cut trees. The aluminum poles make a very useful and roomy geodesic shape, and the fabric is truly watertight. When I bought my current tent I inquired of the salesperson about seam sealing. I was told that is no longer needed, and indeed it is not! I stayed awake quite a while in my first rain with this tent and not a drop came in anywhere and it is light and packs well. This technology evolved just over the past few decades and now is a real boon to modern outdoor camp life.

Figure 12. A modern, light weight, strong, waterproof, and bug proof tent (this one is L. L. Bean's two person Mountain Light).

This tent construction essentially eliminates all the problems that Thoreau experienced sleeping under his 'sheet' a.k.a. a 'Tarp' tent. And it is warm for at least three seasons if used sensibly. For the author, this one was a lifetime in coming and is wonderful in fair and foul weather! When turning in for the night during bug season, it is necessary to kill all bugs that turn in with you. This task typically takes five to eight minutes with a good flashlight*, but then the sleep is wonderful!

---

*Note: discard all old flashlights before embarking on wilderness travel and each person should have two bright LED lights as they are brighter and last longer on smaller batteries. Bring fresh, spare batteries on each trip.

12. July 29- Allagash, Webster Pond, 10 Mile Portage, Tragedy

… and found that he was following his steps backward. I could only occasionally perceive his trail in the moss, and yet he did not appear to look down nor hesitate an instant, but led us out exactly to his canoe.

When we awoke it had done raining, though it was still cloudy. The fire was put out, and the Indian's boots, which stood under the eaves of the tent, were half full of water. He was much more improvident in such respects than either of us, and he had to thank us for keeping his powder dry. We decided to cross the lake at once, before breakfast, or while we could; and before starting I took the bearing of the shore which we wished to strike, S. S. E. about three miles distant, lest a sudden misty rain should conceal it when we were midway. Though the bay in which we were was perfectly quiet and smooth, we found the lake already wide awake outside, but not dangerously or unpleasantly so; nevertheless, when you get out on one of those lakes in a canoe like this, you do not forget that you are completely at the mercy of the wind, and a fickle power it is. The playful waves may at any time become too rude for you in their sport, and play right on over you. We saw a few shecorways and a fish hawk thus early, and after much steady paddling and dancing over the dark waves of Apmoojenegamook, we found ourselves in the neighborhood of the southern land, heard the waves breaking on it, and turned our thoughts wholly to that side. After coasting eastward along this shore a mile or two, we breakfasted on a rocky point, the first convenient place that offered.

It was well enough that we crossed thus early, for the waves now ran quite high, and we should have been obliged to go round somewhat, but beyond this point we had comparatively smooth water. You can commonly go along one side or the other of a lake, when you cannot cross it.

The Indian was looking at the hard-wood ridges from time to time, and said that he would like to buy a few hundred acres somewhere about this lake, asking our advice. It was to buy as near the crossing-place as possible.

My companion and I, having a minute's discussion on some point of ancient history, were amused by the attitude which the Indian, who could not tell what we were talking about, assumed. He constituted himself umpire, and, judging by our air and gesture, he very seriously remarked from time to time, "you beat," or "he beat."

Leaving a spacious bay, a northeasterly prolongation of Chamberlain Lake, on our left, we entered through a short strait into a small lake a couple of miles over, called on the map Telasinis, but the Indian had no distinct name for it, and thence into Telos Lake, which he called Paytaywecomgomoc, or Burnt- Ground Lake. This curved round toward the northeast, and may have been three or four miles long as we paddled. He had not been here since 1825. He did not know what Telos meant; thought it was not Indian. He used the word "spokelogan" (for an inlet in the shore which led nowhere), and when I asked its meaning said that there was "no Indian in 'em." There was a clearing, with a house and barn, on the southwest shore, temporarily occupied by some men who were getting the hay, as we had been told; also a clearing for a pasture on a hill on the west side of the lake.

We landed on a rocky point on the northeast side, to look at some red pines (*Pinus resinosa*), the first we had noticed, and get some cones, for our few which grow in Concord do not bear any.

The outlet from the lake into the East Branch of the Penobscot is an artificial one, and it was not very apparent where it was exactly, but the lake ran curving far up northeasterly into two narrow valleys or ravines, as if it had for a long time been groping its way toward the Penobscot waters, or remembered when it anciently flowed there; by observing where the horizon was lowest, and following the longest of these, we at length reached the dam, having come about a dozen miles from the last camp.

This canal, so called, was a considerable and extremely rapid and rocky river. The Indian decided that there was water enough in it without raising the dam, which would only make it more violent, and that he would run down it alone, while we carried the greater part of the baggage. Our provision being about half consumed, there was the less left in the canoe. We had thrown away the pork-keg, and wrapt its contents in birch bark, which is the unequaled wrapping-paper of the woods.

Following a moist trail through the forest, we reached the head of Webster Pond about the same time with the Indian, notwithstanding the velocity with which he moved, our route being the most direct. The Indian name of Webster

Stream, of which this pond is the source, is, according to him, Madunkchunk, i. e., Height of Land, and of the pond, Madunkchunk-gamooc, or Height of Land Pond. The latter was two or three miles long. We passed near a pine on its shore which had been splintered by lightning, perhaps the day before. This was the first proper East Branch Penobscot water that we came to.

At the outlet of Webster Lake was another dam, at which we stopped and picked raspberries, while the Indian went down the stream a half-mile through the forest, to see what he had got to contend with. There was a deserted log camp here, apparently used the previous winter, with its "hovel" or barn for cattle. In the hut was a large fir twig bed, raised two feet from the floor, occupying a large part of the single apartment, a long narrow table against the wall, with a stout log bench before it, and above the table a small window, the only one there was, which admitted a feeble light. It was a simple and strong fort erected against the cold, and suggested what valiant trencher work had been done there. I discovered one or two curious wooden traps, which had not been used for a long time, in the woods near by. The principal part consisted of a long and slender pole.

An Indian at Oldtown had told us that we should be obliged to carry ten miles between Telos Lake on the St. John and Second Lake on the East Branch of the Penobscot; but the lumberers whom we met assured us that there would not be more than a mile of carry. It turned out that the Indian [from Oldtown], who had lately been over this route, was nearest right, as far as we were concerned. However, if one of us could have assisted the Indian in managing the canoe in the rapids, we might have run the greater part of the way; but as he was alone in the management of the canoe in such places, we were obliged to walk the greater part. I did not feel quite ready to try such an experiment on Webster Stream, which has so bad a reputation. According to my observation, a batteau, properly manned, shoots rapids as a matter of course, which a single Indian with a canoe carries round.

My companion and I carried a good part of the baggage on our shoulders, while the Indian took that which would be least injured by wet in the canoe. We did not know when we should see him again, for he had not been this way since the canal was cut, nor for more than thirty years. He agreed to stop when he got to smooth water, come up and find our path if he could, and halloo for us, and after waiting a reasonable time go on and try again,—and we were to look out in like manner for him.

He commenced by running through the sluiceway and over the dam, as usual, standing up in his tossing canoe, and was soon out of sight behind a point in a wild gorge. This Webster Stream is well known to lumbermen as a difficult one. It is exceedingly rapid and rocky, and also shallow, and can hardly be considered navigable, unless that may mean that what is launched in it is sure to be carried swiftly down it, though it may be dashed to pieces by the way. It is somewhat like navigating a thunder-spout. With commonly an irresistible force urging you on, you have got to choose your own course each moment, between the rocks and shallows, and to get into it, moving forward always with the utmost possible moderation, and often holding on, if you can, that you may inspect the rapids before you.

By the Indian's direction we took an old path on the south side, which appeared to keep down the stream, though at a considerable distance from it, cutting off bends, perhaps to Second Lake, having first taken the course from the map with a compass, which was northeasterly, for safety. It was a wild wood-path, with a few tracks of oxen which had been driven over it, probably to some old camp clearing, for pasturage, mingled with the tracks of moose which had lately used it. We kept on steadily for about an hour without putting down our packs, occasionally winding around or climbing over a fallen tree, for the most part far out of sight and hearing of the river; till, after walking about three miles, we were glad to find that the path came to the river again at an old camp ground, where there was a small opening in the forest, at which we paused. Swiftly as the shallow and rocky river ran here, a continuous rapid with dancing waves, I saw, as I sat on the shore, a long string of sheldrakes, which something scared, run up the opposite side of the stream by me, with the same ease that they commonly did down it, just touching the surface of the waves, and getting an impulse from them as they flowed from under them; but they soon came back, driven by the Indian, who had fallen a little behind us on account of the windings. He shot round a point just above, and came to land by us with considerable water in his canoe. He had found it, as he said, "very strong water," and had been obliged to land once before to empty out what he had taken in. He complained that it strained him to paddle so hard in order to keep his canoe straight in its course, having no one in the bows to aid him, and, shallow as it was, said that it would be no joke to upset there, for the force of the water was such that he had as lief I would strike him over the head with a paddle as have that water strike him. Seeing him come out of that gap was as if you should pour water down an inclined and zigzag trough, then drop a nutshell into it, and, taking a short cut to the bottom, get there in time to see it come out, notwithstanding the rush and tumult, right side up, and only partly full of water.

After a moment's breathing-space, while I held his canoe, he was soon out of sight again around another bend, and we, shouldering our packs, resumed our course.

We did not at once fall into our path again, but made our way with difficulty along the edge of the river, till at length, striking inland through the forest, we recovered it. Before going a mile we heard the Indian calling to us. He had come up through the woods and along the path to find us, having reached sufficiently smooth water to warrant his taking us in. The shore was about one fourth of a mile distant, through a dense, dark forest, and as he led us back to it, winding rapidly about to the right and left, I had the curiosity to look down carefully, and found that he was following his steps backward. I could only occasionally perceive his trail in the moss, and yet he did not appear to look down nor hesitate an instant, but led us out exactly to his canoe. This surprised me; for without a compass, or the sight or noise of the river to guide us, we could not have kept our course many minutes, and could have retraced our steps but a short distance, with a great deal of pains and very slowly, using a laborious circumspection. But it was evident that he could go back through the forest wherever he had been during the day.

As we thus swept along, our Indian repeated in a deliberate and drawling tone the words "Daniel Webster, great lawyer," apparently reminded of him by the name of the stream, and he described his calling on him once in Boston, at what he supposed was his boarding-house. He had no business with him, but merely went to pay his respects, as we should say. In answer to our questions, he described his person well enough. It was on the day after Webster delivered his Bunker Hill oration, which I believe Polis heard. The first time he called he waited till he was tired without seeing him, and then went away. The next time, he saw him go by the door of the room in which he was waiting several times, in his shirt-sleeves, without noticing him. He thought that if he had come to see Indians, they would not have treated him so. At length, after very long delay, he came in, walked toward him, and asked in a loud voice, gruffly, "What do you want?" and he, thinking at first, by the motion of his hand, that he was going to strike him, said to himself, "You'd better take care; if you try that I shall know what to do." He did not like him, and declared that all he said "was not worth talk about a musquash." We suggested that probably Mr. Webster was very busy, and had a great many visitors just then.

Coming to falls and rapids, our easy progress was suddenly terminated. The Indian went alongshore to inspect the water, while we climbed over the rocks, picking berries. The peculiar growth of blueberries on the tops of large rocks here made the impression of high land, and indeed this was the Height-of- Land Stream. When the Indian came back, he remarked, "You got to walk; ver strong water." So, taking out his canoe, he launched it again below the falls, and was soon out of sight. At such times he would step into the canoe, take up his paddle, and, with an air of mystery, start off, looking far down-stream, and keeping his own counsel, as if absorbing all the intelligence of forest and stream into himself; but I sometimes detected a little fun in his face, which could yield to my sympathetic smile, for he was thoroughly good-humored. We meanwhile

Figure 13. A common and local slate-like stone (but softer) found through out the region, but not on Mt. Kineo.

scrambled along the shore with our packs,

without any path. This was the last of our boating for the day.

The prevailing rock here was a kind of slate, standing on its edges and my companion, who was recently from California, thought it exactly like that in which the gold is found, and said that if he had had a pan he would have liked to wash a little of the sand here.

The Indian now got along much faster than we, and waited for us from time to time. I found here the only cool spring that I drank at anywhere on this excursion, a little water filling a hollow in the sandy bank. It was a quite memorable event, and due to the elevation of the country, for wherever else we had been the water in the rivers and the streams emptying in was dead and warm, compared with that of a mountainous region. It was very bad walking along the shore over fallen and drifted trees and bushes, and rocks, from time to time swinging ourselves round over the water, or else taking to a gravel bar or going inland. At one place, the Indian being ahead, I was obliged to take off all my clothes in order to ford a small but deep stream emptying in, while my companion, who was inland, found a rude bridge, high up in the woods, and I saw no more of him for some time. I saw there very fresh moose tracks, found a new goldenrod to me (perhaps *Solidago thyrsoidea*), and I passed one white pine log, which had lodged, in the forest near the edge of the stream, which was quite five feet in diameter at the butt. Probably its size detained it.

Shortly after this I overtook the Indian at the edge of some burnt land, which extended three or four miles at least, beginning about three miles above Second Lake, which we were expecting to reach that night, and which is about ten miles from Telos Lake. This burnt region was still more rocky than before, but, though comparatively open, we could not yet see the lake. Not having seen my companion for some time, I climbed, with the Indian, a singular high rock on the edge of the river, forming a narrow ridge only a foot or two wide at top, in order to look for him; and, after calling many times, I at length heard him answer from a considerable distance inland, he having taken a trail which led off from the river, perhaps directly to the lake, and was now in search of the river again. Seeing a much higher rock, of the same character, about one third of a mile farther east, or down-stream, I proceeded toward it, through the burnt land, in order to look for the lake from its summit, supposing that the Indian would keep down the stream in his canoe, and hallooing all the while that my companion might join me on the way. Before we came together I noticed where a moose, which possibly I had scared by my shouting, had apparently just run along a large rotten trunk of a pine, which made a bridge, thirty or forty feet long, over a hollow, as convenient for him as for me. The tracks were as large as those of an ox, but an ox could not have crossed there. This burnt land was an exceedingly wild and desolate region. Judging by the weeds and sprouts, it appeared to have been burnt about two years before. It was covered with charred trunks, either prostrate or standing, which crocked our clothes and hands, and we could not easily have distinguished a bear there by his color. Great shells of trees, sometimes unburnt without, or burnt on one side only, but black within, stood twenty or forty feet high. The fire had run up inside, as in a chimney, leaving the sap-wood. Sometimes we crossed a rocky ravine fifty feet wide, on a fallen trunk; and there were great fields of fire-weed *(Epilobium angustifolium)* on all sides, the most extensive that I ever saw, which presented great masses of pink. Intermixed with these were blueberry and raspberry bushes.

Having crossed a second rocky ridge like the first, when I was beginning to ascend the third, the Indian, whom I had left on the shore some fifty rods behind, beckoned to me to come to him, but I made sign that I would first ascend the highest rock before me, whence I expected to see the lake. My companion accompanied me to the top. This was formed just like the others. Being struck with the perfect parallelism of these singular rock hills, however much one might be in advance of another, I took out my compass and found that they lay northwest and southeast, the rock being on its edge, and sharp edges they were. This one, to speak from memory, was perhaps a third of a mile in length, but quite narrow, rising gradually from the northwest to the height of about eighty feet, but steep on the southeast end. The southwest side was as steep as an ordinary roof, or as we could safely climb; the northeast was an abrupt precipice from which you could jump clean to the bottom, near which the river flowed; while the level top of the ridge, on which you walked along, was only from one to three or four feet in width. For a rude illustration, take the half of a pear cut in two lengthwise, lay it on its flat side, the stem to the northwest, and then halve it vertically in the direction of its length, keeping the southwest half. Such was the general form.

There was a remarkable series of these great rock-waves revealed by the burning; breakers, as it were. No wonder that the river that found its way through them was rapid and obstructed by falls. No doubt the absence of soil on these rocks, or its dryness where there was any, caused this to be a very thorough burning. We could see the lake over the woods, two or three miles ahead, and that the river made an abrupt turn southward around the northwest end of the cliff on which we stood, or a little above us, so that we had cut off a bend, and that there was an important fall in it a short distance below us. I could see the canoe a hundred rods behind, but now on the opposite shore, and supposed that the Indian had concluded to take out and carry round some bad rapids on that side, and that that might be what he had beckoned to me for; but after waiting a while I could still see nothing of him, and I observed to my companion that I wondered where he was, though I began to suspect that he had gone inland to look for the lake from some hilltop on that side, as we had done. This proved to be the case; for after I had started to return to the canoe, I heard a faint halloo, and descried him on the top of a distant rocky hill on that side. But as, after a long time had elapsed, I still saw his canoe in the same place, and he had not returned to it, and appeared in no hurry to do so, and, moreover, as I remembered that he had previously beckoned to me, I thought that there might be something more to delay him than I knew, and began to return northwest, along the ridge, toward the angle in the river. My companion, who had just been separated from us, and had even contemplated the necessity of camping alone, wishing to husband his steps, and yet to keep with us, inquired where I was going; to which I answered that I was going far enough back to communicate with the Indian, and that then I thought we had better go along the shore together, and keep him in sight.

When we reached the shore, the Indian appeared from out the woods on the opposite side, but on account of the roar of the water it was difficult to communicate with him. He kept along the shore westward to his canoe, while we stopped at the angle where the stream turned southward around the precipice. I again said to my companion that we would keep along the shore and keep the Indian in sight. We started to do so, being close together, the Indian behind us having launched his canoe again, but just then I saw the latter, who had crossed to our side, forty or fifty rods behind, beckoning to me, and I called to my companion, who had just disappeared behind large rocks at the point of the precipice, three or four rods before me, on his way down the stream, that I was going to help the Indian a moment. I did so,—helped get the canoe over a fall, lying with my breast over a rock, and holding one end while he received it below,—and within ten or fifteen minutes at most I was back again at the point where the river turned southward, in order to catch up with my companion, while Polis glided down the river alone, parallel with me. But to my surprise, when I rounded the precipice, though the shore was bare of trees, without rocks, for a quarter of a mile at least, my companion was not to be seen. It was as if he had sunk into the earth. This was the more unaccountable to me, because I knew that his feet were, since our swamp walk, very sore, and that he wished to keep with the party; and besides this was very bad walking, climbing over or about the rocks. I hastened along, hallooing and searching for him, thinking he might be concealed behind a rock, yet doubting if he had not taken the other side of the precipice, but the Indian had got along still faster in his canoe, till he was arrested by the falls, about a quarter of a mile below. He then landed, and said that we could go no farther that night. The sun was setting, and on account of falls and rapids we should be obliged to leave this river and carry a good way into another farther east. The first thing then was to find my companion, for I was now very much alarmed about him, and I sent the Indian along the shore down-stream, which began to be covered with unburnt wood again just below the falls, while I searched backward about the precipice which we had passed. The Indian showed some unwillingness to exert himself, complaining that he was very tired, in consequence of his day's work, that it had strained him very much getting down so many rapids alone; but he went off calling somewhat like an owl. I remembered that my companion was near-sighted, and I feared that he had either fallen from the precipice, or fainted and sunk down amid the rocks beneath it. I shouted and searched above and below this precipice in the twilight till I could not see, expecting nothing less than to find his body beneath it. For half an hour I anticipated and believed only the worst. I thought what I should do the next day if I did not find him, what I could do in such a wilderness, and how his relatives would feel, if I should return without him. I felt that if he were really lost away from the river there, it would be a desperate undertaking to find him; and where were they who could help you? What would it be to raise the country, where there were only two or three camps, twenty or thirty miles apart, and no road, and perhaps nobody at home? Yet we must try the harder, the less the prospect of success.

I rushed down from this precipice to the canoe in order to fire the Indian's gun, but found that my companion had the caps. I was still thinking of getting it off when the Indian returned. He had not found him, but he said that he had seen his tracks once or twice along the shore. This encouraged me very much. He objected to firing the gun, saying that if my companion heard it, which was not likely, on account of the roar of the stream, it would tempt him to come toward us, and he might break his neck in the dark. For the same reason we refrained from lighting a fire on the highest rock. I proposed that we should both keep down the stream to the lake, or that I should go at any rate, but the Indian said: "No use, can't do anything in the dark; come morning, then we find 'em. No harm,—he make 'em camp. No bad animals here, no gristly bears, such as in California, where he's been,—warm night,—he well off as you and I." I considered that if he was well he could do without us. He had just lived eight years in California, and had plenty of experience with wild beasts and wilder men, was peculiarly accustomed to make journeys of great length; but if he were sick or dead, he was near where we were. The darkness in the woods was by this time so thick that it alone decided the question. We must camp where we were. I knew that he had his knapsack, with blankets and matches, and, if well, would fare no worse than we, except that he would have no supper nor society.

This side of the river being so encumbered with rocks, we crossed to the eastern or smoother shore, and proceeded to camp there, within two or three rods of the falls. We pitched no tent, but lay on the sand, putting a few handfuls of grass and twigs under us, there being no evergreen at hand. For fuel we had some of the charred stumps. Our various bags of provisions had got quite wet in the rapids, and I arranged them about the fire to dry. The fall close by was the principal one on this stream, and it shook the earth under us. It was a cool, because dewy, night; the more so, probably, owing to the nearness of the falls. The Indian complained a good deal, and thought afterward that he got a cold there which occasioned a more serious illness. We were not much troubled by mosquitoes at any rate. I lay awake a good deal from anxiety, but, unaccountably to myself, was at length comparatively at ease respecting him. At first I had apprehended the worst, but now I had little doubt but that I should find him in the morning. From time to time I fancied that I heard his voice calling through the roar of the falls from the opposite side of the river; but it is doubtful if we could have heard him across the stream there. Sometimes I doubted whether the Indian had really seen his tracks, since he manifested an unwillingness to make much of a search, and then my anxiety returned.

It was the most wild and desolate region we had camped in, where, if anywhere, one might expect to meet with befitting inhabitants, but I heard only the squeak of a nighthawk flitting over. The moon in her first quarter, in the fore part of the night, setting over the bare rocky hills garnished with tall, charred, and hollow stumps or shells of trees, served to reveal the desolation.

Comments:

Leaving the Allagash, Thoreau commented:

> We decided to cross the lake at once, before breakfast, or while we could; and before starting I took the bearing of the shore which we wished to strike, S. S. E. about three miles distant, lest a sudden misty rain should conceal it when we were midway.

He was using his map and compass as they should be used.

And then when they started the 10-mile carry, he comments:

> having first taken the course from the map with a compass, which was northeasterly, for safety.

Lesson well learned!

Despite better planning, a freak accident caused the group to be split up and Thoreau observed:

> I thought what I should do the next day if I did not find him, what I could do in such a wilderness, and how his relatives would feel, if I should return without him.

To become a registered Maine guide, one must take a written as well as an oral exam covering many issues, one of which is how to conduct a lost person search. This is what Thoreau and his guide faced that evening:

> *I proposed that we should both keep down the stream to the lake, or that I should go at any rate, but the Indian said: 'No use, can't do anything in the dark; come morning, then we find 'em. No harm,—he make 'em camp. No bad animals here, no gristly bears, such as in California, where he's been,—warm night,—he well off as you and I.'*

This occasion was one of few where the best course of action was to do nothing. This was not the first time Thoreau, and his partner, were lost on this journey. Their handling of such situations in general was not wise. If they had waited in any of these situations, their guide would have found them and given them guidance – that's why he was their guide! But in this case at this moment, Joe Polis called it exactly right.

13. July 30- Matungamook (Matagamon), Homeward

He thought it likely that he had heard the Indian call once the evening before, but mistook it for an owl.

It was not apparent where the outlet of this lake was, and while the Indian thought it was in one direction, I thought it was in another. He said, "I bet you four-pence it is there," but he still held on in my direction, which proved to be the right one.

I aroused the Indian early this morning to go in search of our companion, expecting to find him within a mile or two, farther down the stream. The Indian wanted his breakfast first, but I reminded him that my companion had had neither breakfast nor supper. We were obliged first to carry our canoe and baggage over into another stream, the main East Branch, about three fourths of a mile distant, for Webster Stream was no farther navigable. We went twice over this carry, and the dewy bushes wet us through like water up to the middle; I hallooed in a high key from time to time, though I had little expectation that I could be heard over the roar of the rapids, and, moreover, we were necessarily on the opposite side of the stream to him. In going over this portage the last time, the Indian, who was before me with the canoe on his head, stumbled and fell heavily once, and lay for a moment silent, as if in pain. I hastily stepped forward to help him, asking if he was much hurt, but after a moment's pause, without replying, he sprang up and went forward. He was all the way subject to taciturn fits, but they were harmless ones.

We had launched our canoe and gone but little way down the East Branch, when I heard an answering shout from my companion, and soon after saw him standing on a point where there was a clearing a quarter of a mile below, and the smoke of his fire was rising near by. Before I saw him I naturally shouted again and again, but the Indian curtly remarked, "He hears you," as if once was enough. It was just below the mouth of Webster Stream. When we arrived, he was smoking his pipe, and said that he had passed a pretty comfortable night, though it was rather cold, on account of the dew.

It appeared that when we stood together the previous evening, and I was shouting to the Indian across the river, he, being near-sighted, had not seen the Indian nor his canoe, and when I went back to the Indian's assistance, did not see which way I went, and supposed that we were below and not above him, and so, making haste to catch up, he ran away from us. Having reached this clearing, a mile or more below our camp, the night overtook him, and he made a fire in a little hollow, and lay down by it in his blanket, still thinking that we were ahead of him. He thought it likely that he had heard the Indian call once the evening before, but mistook it for an owl. He had seen one botanical rarity before it was dark,— pure white *Epilobium angustifolium* amidst the fields of pink ones, in the burnt lands. He had already stuck up the remnant of a lumberer's shirt, found on the point, on a pole by the waterside, for a signal, and attached a note to it, to inform us that he had gone on to the lake, and that if he did not find us there, he would be back in a couple of hours. If he had not found us soon, he had some thoughts of going back in search of the solitary hunter whom we had met at Telos Lake, ten miles behind, and, if successful, hire him to take him to Bangor. But if this hunter had moved as fast as we, he would have been twenty miles off by this time, and who could guess in what direction? It would have been like looking for a needle in a haymow, to search for him in these woods. He had been considering how long he could live on berries alone.

We substituted for his note a card containing our names and destination, and the date of our visit, which Polis neatly inclosed in a piece of birch bark to keep it dry. This has probably been read by some hunter or explorer ere this.

We all had good appetites for the breakfast which we made haste to cook here, and then, having partially dried our clothes, we glided swiftly down the winding stream toward Second Lake.

As the shores became flatter with frequent gravel and sand-bars, and the stream more winding in the lower land near the lake, elms and ash trees made their appearance; also the wild yellow lily (*Lilium Canadense*), some of whose bulbs I collected for a soup. On some ridges the burnt land extended as far as the lake. This was a very beautiful lake, two or three miles long, with high mountains on the southwest side, the (as our Indian said) Nerlumskeechticook, i.e., Deadwater Mountain. It appears to be the same called Carbuncle Mountain on the map. According to Polis, it extends in separate elevations all along this and the next lake, which is much larger. The lake, too, I think, is called by the same name, or perhaps with the addition of gamoc or mooc. The morning was a bright one, and perfectly still and serene, the lake as smooth as glass, we making the only ripple as we paddled into it. The dark mountains about it were seen through a glaucous mist, and the brilliant white stems of canoe birches mingled with the other woods around it. The wood thrush sang on the distant shore, and the laugh of some loons, sporting in a concealed western bay, as if inspired by the morning, came distinct over the lake to us, and, what was more remarkable, the echo which ran round the lake was much louder than the original note; probably because, the loon being in a regularly curving bay under the mountain, we were exactly in the focus of many echoes, the sound being reflected like light from a concave mirror. The beauty of the scene may have been enhanced to our eyes by the fact that we had just come together again after a night of some anxiety. This reminded me of the Ambejijis Lake on the West Branch, which I crossed in my first coming to Maine. Having paddled down three quarters of the lake, we came to a standstill, while my companion let down for fish. A white (or whitish) gull sat on a rock which rose above the surface in mid-lake not far off, quite in harmony with the scene; and as we rested there in the warm sun, we heard one loud crushing or crackling sound from the forest, forty or fifty rods distant, as of a stick broken by the foot of some large animal. Even this was an interesting incident there. In the midst of our dreams of giant lake trout, even then supposed to be nibbling, our fishermen drew up a diminutive red perch, and we took up our paddles again in haste.

It was not apparent where the outlet of this lake was, and while the Indian thought it was in one direction, I thought it was in another. He said, "I bet you four-pence it is there," but he still held on in my direction, which proved to be the right one. As we were approaching the outlet, it being still early in the forenoon, he suddenly exclaimed, "Moose! moose!" and told us to be still. He put a cap on his gun, and, standing up in the stern, rapidly pushed the canoe straight toward the shore and the moose. It was a cow moose, about thirty rods off, standing in the water by the side of the outlet, partly behind some fallen timber and bushes, and at that distance she did not look very large. She was flapping her large ears, and from time to time poking off the flies with her nose from some part of her body. She did not appear much alarmed by our neighborhood, only occasionally turned her head and looked straight at us, and then gave her attention to the flies again. As we approached nearer she got out of the water, stood higher, and regarded us more suspiciously. Polis pushed the canoe steadily forward in the shallow water, and I for a moment forgot the moose in attending to some pretty rose-colored *Polygonums* just rising above the surface, but the canoe soon grounded in the mud eight or ten rods distant from the moose, and the Indian seized his gun and prepared to fire. After standing still a moment, she turned slowly, as usual, so as to expose her side, and he improved this moment to fire, over our heads. She thereupon moved off eight or ten rods at a moderate pace, across a shallow bay, to an old standing-place of hers, behind some fallen red maples, on the opposite shore, and there she stood still again a dozen or fourteen rods from us, while the Indian hastily loaded and fired twice at her, without her moving. My companion, who passed him his caps and bullets, said that Polis was as excited as a boy of fifteen, that his hand trembled, and he once put his ramrod back upside down. This was remarkable for so experienced a hunter. Perhaps he was anxious to make a good shot before us. The white hunter had told me that the Indians were not good shots, because they were excited, though he said that we had got a good hunter with us.

The Indian now pushed quickly and quietly back, and a long distance round, in order to get into the outlet,—for he had fired over the neck of a peninsula between it and the lake,—till we approached the place where the moose had stood, when he exclaimed, "She is a goner!" and was surprised that we did not see her as soon as he did. There, to be sure, she lay perfectly dead, with her tongue hanging out, just where she had stood to receive the last shots, looking unexpectedly large and horse-like, and we saw where the bullets had scarred the trees.

Using a tape, I found that the moose measured just six feet from the shoulder to the tip of the hoof, and was eight feet long as she lay. Some portions of the body, for a foot in diameter, were almost covered with flies, apparently the common fly of our woods, with a dark spot on the wing, and not the very large ones which occasionally pursued us in midstream, though both are called moose-flies.

Polis, preparing to skin the moose, asked me to help him find a stone on which to sharpen his large knife. It being all a flat alluvial ground where the moose had fallen, covered with red maples, etc., this was no easy matter; we searched far and wide, a long time, till at length I found a flat kind of slate-stone, and soon after he returned with a similar one, on which he soon made his knife very sharp.

Figure 14. Moose are prevalent today along the Thoreau journey route; this one was seen on the West Branch where Polis was keeping a sharp eye out for an opportunity to shoot one. He got his wish later, on the East Branch.

While he was skinning the moose, I proceeded to ascertain what kind of fishes were to be found in the sluggish and muddy outlet. The greatest difficulty was to find a pole. It was almost impossible to find a slender, straight pole ten or twelve feet long in those woods. You might search half an hour in vain. They are commonly spruce, arbor-vitæ, fir, etc., short, stout, and branchy, and do not make good fish-poles, even after you have patiently cut off all their tough and scraggy branches. The fishes were red perch and chivin.

The Indian, having cut off a large piece of sirloin, the upper lip, and the tongue, wrapped them in the hide, and placed them in the bottom of the canoe, observing that there was "one man," meaning the weight of one. Our load had previously been reduced some thirty pounds, but a hundred pounds were now added,—a serious addition, which made our quarters still more narrow, and considerably increased the danger on the lakes and rapids, as well as the labor of the carries. The skin was ours according to custom, since the Indian was in our employ, but we did not think of claiming it. He being a skillful dresser of moose-hides would make it worth seven or eight dollars to him, as I was told. He said that he sometimes earned fifty or sixty dollars in a day at them; he had killed ten moose in one day, though the skinning and all took two days. This was the way he had got his property. There were the tracks of a calf thereabouts, which he said would come "by, by," and he could get it if we cared to wait, but I cast cold water on the project.

We continued along the outlet toward Grand Lake, through a swampy region, by a long, winding, and narrow dead water, very much choked up by wood, where we were obliged to land sometimes in order to get the canoe over a log. It was hard to find any channel, and we did not know but we should be lost in the swamp. It abounded in ducks, as usual. At length we reached Grand Lake, which the Indian called Matungamook.

At the head of this we saw, coming in from the southwest, with a sweep apparently from a gorge in the mountains, Trout Stream, or Uncardnerheese, which name, the Indian said, had something to do with mountains.

We stopped to dine on an interesting high rocky island, soon after entering Matungamook Lake, securing our canoe to the cliffy shore. It is always pleasant to step from a boat on to a large rock or cliff. Here was a good opportunity to dry our dewy blankets on the open sunny rock. Indians had recently camped here, and accidentally burned over the western end of the island, and Polis picked up a gun-case of blue broadcloth, and said that he knew the Indian it belonged to, and would carry it to him. His tribe is not so large but he may know all its effects. We proceeded to make a fire and cook our dinner amid some pines, where our predecessors had done the same, while the Indian busied himself about his moose-hide on the shore, for he said that he thought it a good plan for one to do all the cooking, i. e., I suppose, if that one were not himself. A peculiar evergreen overhung our fire, which at first glance looked like a pitch pine (*P. rigida*), with leaves little more than an inch long, spruce-like, but we found it to be the *Pinus Banksiana*,—"Banks's, or the Labrador Pine," also called scrub pine, gray pine, etc., a new tree to us. These must have been good specimens, for several were thirty or thirty-five feet high. Richardson found it forty feet high and upward, and states that the porcupine feeds on its bark. Here also grew the red pine (*Pinus resinosa*).

I saw where the Indians had made canoes in a little secluded hollow in the woods, on the top of the rock, where they were out of the wind, and large piles of whittlings remained. This must have been a favorite resort for their ancestors, and, indeed, we found here the point of an arrowhead, such as they have not used for two centuries and now know not how to make. The Indian, picking up a stone, remarked to me, "That very strange lock (rock)." It was a piece of hornstone, which I told him his tribe had probably brought here centuries before to make arrowheads of. He also picked up a yellowish curved bone by the side of our fireplace and asked me to guess what it was. It was one of the upper incisors of a beaver, on which some party had feasted within a year or two. I found also most of the teeth, and the skull, etc. We here dined on fried moose-meat.

One who was my companion in my two previous excursions to these woods, tells me that when hunting up the Caucomgomoc, about two years ago, he found himself dining one day on moose-meat, mud turtle, trout, and beaver, and he thought that there were few places in the world where these dishes could easily be brought together on one table.

After the almost incessant rapids and falls of the Madunkchunk (Height-of- Land, or Webster Stream), we had just passed through the dead water of Second Lake, and were now in the much larger dead water of Grand Lake, and I thought the Indian was entitled to take an extra nap here. Ktaadn, near which we were to pass the next day, is said to mean "Highest Land." So much geography is there in their names. The Indian navigator naturally distinguishes by a name those parts of a stream where he has encountered quick water and forks, and again, the lakes and smooth water where he can rest his weary arms, since those are the most interesting and more arable parts to him. The very sight of the Nerlumskeechticook, or Deadwater Mountains, a day's journey off over the forest, as we first saw them, must awaken in him pleasing memories. And not less interesting is it to the white traveler, when he is crossing a placid lake in these out-of-the-way woods, perhaps thinking that he is in some sense one of the earlier discoverers of it, to be reminded that it was thus well known and suitably named by Indian hunters perhaps a thousand years ago.

Ascending the precipitous rock which formed this long narrow island, I was surprised to find that its summit was a narrow ridge, with a precipice on one side, and that its axis of elevation extended from northwest to southeast exactly like that of the great rocky ridge at the commencement of the Burnt Ground, ten miles northwesterly. The same arrangement prevailed here, and we could plainly see that the mountain ridges on the west of the lake trended the same way. Splendid large harebells nodded over the edge and in the clefts of the cliff, and the blueberries (*Vaccinium Canadense*) were for the first time really abundant in the thin soil on its top. There was no lack of them henceforward on the East Branch. There was a fine view hence over the sparkling lake, which looked pure and deep, and had two or three, in all, rocky islands in it. Our blankets being dry, we set out again, the Indian as usual having left his gazette on a tree. This time it was we three in a canoe, my companion smoking. We paddled southward down this handsome lake, which appeared to extend nearly as far east as south, keeping near the western shore, just outside a small island, under the dark Nerlumskeechticook Mountain. For I had observed on my map that this was the course. It was three or four miles across it. It struck me that the outline of this mountain on the southwest of the lake, and of another beyond it, was not only like that of the huge rock waves of Webster Stream, but in the main like Kineo, on Moosehead Lake, having a similar but less abrupt precipice at the southeast end; in short, that all the prominent hills and ridges hereabouts were larger or smaller Kineos, and that possibly there was such a relation between Kineo and the rocks of Webster Stream.

The Indian did not know exactly where the outlet was, whether at the extreme southwest angle or more easterly, and had asked to see my plan at the last stopping-place, but I had forgotten to show it to him. As usual, he went feeling his way by a middle course between two probable points, from which he could diverge either way at last without losing much distance. In approaching the south shore, as the clouds looked gusty and the waves ran pretty high, we so steered as to get partly under the lee of an island, though at a great distance from it.

I could not distinguish the outlet till we were almost in it, and heard the water falling over the dam there.

Here was a considerable fall, and a very substantial dam, but no sign of a cabin or camp. The hunter whom we met at Telos Lake had told us that there were plenty of trout here, but at this hour they did not rise to the bait, only cousin trout, from the very midst of the rushing waters. There are not so many fishes in these rivers as in the Concord.

While we loitered here, Polis took occasion to cut with his big knife some of the hair from his moose-hide, and so lightened and prepared it for drying. I noticed at several old Indian camps in the woods the pile of hair which they had cut from their hides.

Having carried over the dam, he darted down the rapids, leaving us to walk for a mile or more, where for the most part there was no path, but very thick and difficult traveling near the stream. At length he would call to let us know where he was waiting for us with his canoe, when, on account of the windings of the stream, we did not know where the shore was, but he did not call often enough, forgetting that we were not Indians. He seemed to be very saving of his breath,—yet he would be surprised if we went by, or did not strike the right spot. This was not because he was unaccommodating, but a proof of superior manners. Indians like to get along with the least possible communication and ado. He was really paying us a great compliment all the while, thinking that we preferred a hint to a kick.

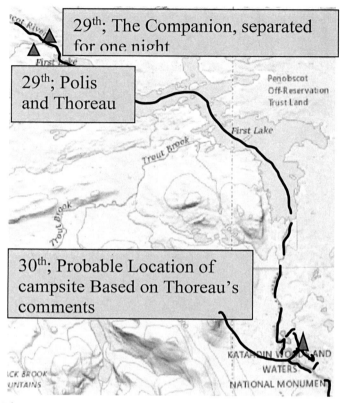

Fig. 15. End of 10-mile portage, Grand Lake Matagamon, and the entering the East Branch of the Penobscot heading towards Indian Island

It is surprising on stepping ashore anywhere into this unbroken wilderness to see so often, at least within a few rods of the river, the marks of the axe, made by lumberers who have either camped here or driven logs past in previous springs. You will see perchance where, going on the same errand that you do, they have cut large chips from a tall white pine stump for their fire. While we were pitching the camp and getting supper, the Indian cut the rest of the hair from his moose-hide, and proceeded to extend it vertically on a temporary frame between two small trees, half a dozen feet from the opposite side of the fire, lashing and stretching it with arbor-vitæ bark which was always at hand, and in this case was stripped from one of the trees it was tied to. Asking for a new kind of tea, he made us some, pretty good, of the checkerberry (*Gaultheria procumbens*), which covered the ground, dropping a little bunch of it tied up with cedar bark into the kettle; but it was not quite equal to the Chiogenes. We called this therefore Checkerberry-Tea Camp.

I was struck with the abundance of the *Linnœa borealis*, checkerberry, and *Chiogenes hispidula*, almost everywhere in the Maine woods. The wintergreen (*Chimaphila umbellata*) was still in bloom here, and clintonia berries were abundant and ripe. This handsome plant is one of the most common in that forest. We here first noticed the moose-wood in fruit on the banks. The prevailing trees were spruce (commonly black), arbor-vitæ, canoe birch (black ash and elms beginning to appear), yellow birch, red maple, and a little hemlock skulking in the forest. The Indian said that the white maple punk was the best for tinder, that yellow birch punk was pretty good, but hard. After supper he put on the moose tongue and lips to boil, cutting out the septum. He showed me how to write on the under side of birch bark, with a black spruce twig, which is hard and tough, and can be brought to a point.

The Indian wandered off into the woods a short distance just before night, and, coming back, said, "Me found great treasure,—fifty, sixty dollars' worth."

"What's that?" we asked. "Steel traps, under a log, thirty or forty, I didn't count 'em. I guess Indian work,—worth three dollars apiece." It was a singular coincidence that he should have chanced to walk to and look under that particular log, in that trackless forest.

Tonight the Indian lay between the fire and his stretched moose-hide, to avoid the mosquitoes. Indeed, he also made a small smoky fire of damp leaves at his head and his feet, and then as usual rolled up his head in his blanket. We with our veils and our wash were tolerably comfortable, but it would be difficult to pursue any sedentary occupation in the woods at this season; you cannot see to read much by the light of a fire through a veil in the evening, nor handle pencil and paper well with gloves or anointed fingers.

Comments:

After the party reunited and had breakfast together, the trip then proceeded. The rest of the day didn't have as much excitement as others, but one can learn from his moose hunting (a good shot at quite some distance), hide preparation, navigating in unknown lake water, and making herbal teas in the Maine Woods and much more.

The first lesson of the day involves the companion's inclination to start out on his own if he did not encounter Polis and Thoreau within a few hours. Recall that they slept at different sites and woke up not knowing where each other was to be found. The stated facts of this dangerous impulse point to a likely tragic disaster if they had not quickly found each other – it was good that Thoreau refused breakfast until they were reunited. This potential disaster would have ruined the entire trip with death likely resulting.

I have also been on the same waters of the Matagamon when the weather turned foul for a good period of time. The decision was made to hold tight until better weather, regardless of likely schedule delay and a late return. Later, a passing motorboat operator informed us about several canoes from a different party that had swamped downstream due to a foolish attempt. Blessedly, no one was lost and later that day the winds and waves subsided, and we were able to travel onwards. Caution is always best.

Thoreau may have erred when he tried to identify the new (to him) Pitch Pine versus Pinus Banksiana. Omitted from discussion was the number of needles in each fascicle; Pitch Pine has 3 needles and Banksiana has 2, just like Red Pine, according to various common references. There is no good reason to confuse the two.

Thoreau's mood for the day was tempered by a deeply felt disgust for the killing of the moose. Not only was it a cow moose that could have had a calf to became orphaned, but also while the pelt was used, and that likely for moccasins, much of the meat was lost which was common. The pelts were a lucrative item of trade.

14. *Vignette 4:* Canoes, Paddles, Packing and Portages

Canoes

Canoeing is a serious part of the American wilderness experience whether native or immigrant. It calls of the wild and lifts one's sense of adventure and connection to nature. So, let's look at some of Joe's work with his canoe(s) starting with the one rented by Henry Thoreau.

> It was 18¼ feet long by 2 feet 6½ inches wide in the middle, and one foot deep within, so I (Thoreau) found by measurement, and I judged that it would weigh not far from eighty pounds. The Indian had recently made it himself, and its smallness was partly compensated for by its newness, as well as stanchness and solidity, it being made of very thick bark and ribs. Our baggage weighed about 166 pounds, so that the canoe carried about 600 pounds in all, or the weight of four men. The principal part of the baggage was, as usual, placed in the middle of the broadest part, while we stowed ourselves in the chinks and crannies that were left before and behind it, where there was no room to extend our legs, the loose articles being tucked into the ends. The canoe was thus as closely packed as a market-basket, and might possibly have been upset without spilling any of its contents. The Indian sat on a

cross-bar in the stern, but we flat on the bottom, with a splint or chip behind our backs, to protect them from the cross-bar, and one of us commonly paddled with the Indian.

18' is a good length for three grown men and their gear and hides. I prefer 16' when only two people are traveling and have used such canoes on various parts of this same trip. I have used one 17' canoe for an entire summer and found it to be heavy and cumbersome to carry. The 16' length is lighter, handles well, and is stable in rough weather, with proper handling, and is very suitable for two people. Joe really worked hard in rough weather but the choice between the two lengths comes down to many factors. The biggest difference between the canoe that Joe made, and today's canoe, is in the seats. Modern canoes do have seats whereas Joe's did not, according to the custom of the times. I much prefer having seats but when the weather gets rough, we often get on our knees and paddle with a lower profile. Following safe paddling guidelines and sensible choices keeps the trip safe. The birch canoe, though, has its own peculiarities.

The Indian was always very careful in approaching the shore, lest he should injure his canoe on the rocks, letting it swing round slowly sidewise, and was still more particular that we should not step into it on shore, nor till it floated free, and then should step gently lest we should open its seams, or make a hole in the bottom.

The cautions just given are wise to preserve the integrity of any canoe on any trip.

Again we crossed a broad bay opposite the mouth of Moose River, before reaching the narrow strait at Mount Kineo, made what the voyageurs call a traverse, and found the water quite rough. A very little wind on these broad lakes raises a sea which will swamp a canoe. Looking off from the shore, the surface may appear to be very little agitated, almost smooth, a mile distant, or if you see a few white crests they appear nearly level with the rest of the lake; but when you get out so far, you may find quite a sea running, and ere long, before you think of it, a wave will gently creep up the side of the canoe and fill your lap, like a monster deliberately covering you with its slime before it swallows you, or it will strike the canoe violently, and break into it. The same thing may happen when the wind rises suddenly, though it were perfectly calm and smooth there a few minutes before; so that nothing can save you, unless you can swim ashore, for it is impossible to get into a canoe again when it is upset. Since you sit flat on the bottom, though the danger should not be imminent, a little water is a great inconvenience, not to mention the wetting of your provisions. We rarely crossed even a bay directly, from point to point, when there was wind, but made a slight curve corresponding somewhat to the shore, that we might the sooner reach it if the wind increased.

The Indian paddled on one side, and one of us on the other, to keep the canoe steady, and when he wanted to change hands he would say, "T' other side." He asserted, in answer to our questions, that he had never upset a canoe himself, though he may have been upset by others.

As the forenoon advanced, the wind increased. The last bay which we crossed before reaching the desolate pier at the Northeast Carry was two or three miles over, and the wind was southwesterly. After going a third of the way, the waves had increased so as occasionally to wash into the canoe, and we saw that it was worse and worse ahead. At first we might have turned about, but were not willing to. It would have been of no use to follow the course of the shore, for not only the distance would have been much greater, but the waves ran still higher there on account of the greater sweep the wind had. At any rate it would have been dangerous now to alter our course, because the waves would have struck us at an advantage. It will not do to meet them at right angles, for then they will wash in both sides, but you must take them quartering. So the Indian stood up in the canoe, and exerted all his skill and strength for a mile or two, while I paddled right along in order to give him more steerage-way. For more than a mile he did not allow a single wave to strike the canoe as it would, but turned it quickly from this side to that, so that it would always be on or near the crest of a wave when it broke, where all its force was spent, and we merely settled down with it. At length I jumped out on to the end of the pier, against which the waves were dashing violently, in order to lighten the canoe, and catch it at the landing, which was not much sheltered; but just as I jumped we took in two or three gallons of water. I remarked to the Indian, "You managed that well," to which he replied, "Ver few men do that. Great many waves; when I look out for one, another come quick.

He sometimes, also, went a-hunting to the Seboois Lakes, taking the stage, with his gun and ammunition, axe and blankets, hard-bread and pork, perhaps for a hundred miles of the way, and jumped off at the wildest place on the road, where he was at once at home, and every rod was a tavern-site for him. Then, after a short journey through the woods, he would build a spruce-bark canoe in one day, putting but few ribs into it, that it might be light, and, after doing his hunting with it on the lakes, would return with his furs the same way he had come.

Joe's canoes had ribs and birch bark skin. In the last example of his Seboois ventures he built the canoe in a day using spruce bark. The question is, however, did the canoe for this trip have many ribs made from flat cedar or just a few made likely from rather smaller branches or stems bent into the curvature of the canoe? The former is the nature of modern wood and canvas canoes where the ribs almost touch each other but takes many months of fine woodworking to craft; or did he use very few naturally round ribs bent to shape. Most likely it is the latter because 1) we have a report of his making a canoe in a day and 2) he was very concerned about how people stepped into the canoe so as not to make leaks (not a problem for a canoe with many ribs). It should be noted that Native Americans, over time, used both methods. I visualize the whole trip with the canoe with the simpler construction.

In general, Thoreau's description of Joe's canoe comports well with best practices even today. The North American style canoe originated with native groups and is a wonderful gift to all making for great trips and leisure paddling. And at the end of their trip,

> Polis wanted to sell us his canoe, said it would last seven or eight years, or with care, perhaps ten; but we were not ready to buy it.

This offer of sale was attractive, but not to Thoreau who eschewed possessions in general in favor of a more contemplative life.

Paddles

A second interesting question concerns the

paddles. They seemed to be rather long and the longest was for the stern man. This is not typical of today's canoeing. Typically, the stern paddler has a length that would come up from the ground to a person's chin or nose whereas the bowman would have a longer one that came to

his forehead. This is not the best if the stern man stands up in the canoe to paddle and

Figure 16. Joe's well packed canoe per Thoreau's records. Thoreau is crouched in the bow with little items. The two packs and two India rubber bags are next, and the companion is just aft of the middle thwart, sitting on the floor. In between are the pork barrel, the bread bag and a miscellaneous bag plus the polling pole for shallow waters. The skillet and pot are tucked alongside the companion, plus dippers, with moose hide folded in front of the companion. Joe sits aft with his axe and gun right behind him. The sugar and coffee are likely in the India rubber bags.

the longer paddle is then needed. Joe was recorded as standing up when running with the wind in heavy waves and also going down stream with a strong current. Hence his longer paddle. Standing is not recommended for novices, and it does carry some risk even for experts.

The Polis native practice of having the bowman sitting square on the floor is no doubt the cause of using a longer paddle for the bowman. Indeed, the single greatest canoe difference between 1857 and more modern times is the advent of a proper seat both in the stern and in the bow. Without both seats, contemporary canoeing would be quite uncomfortable.

Packing

Joe Polis packed his canoe much as one does even now; the laws of physics haven't changed in one hundred and sixty-five years! One needs to keep the weight well centered and as close to the bottom as possible.

No one today would even think about eating as was done on this trip. A barrel of pork, a bag of ship hard bread, coffee and sugar were the only foods taken with them. Today one can economically provide a wide choice of foods that can suffice for periods up to about 14 days and all can be packed just as crefully as Polis did in 1857. It is strongly suggested that one improve on dish washing as their practices were risky at best and not very clean at all.

Portaging

The standard practice on this trip was for Polis to portage the canoe alone, which is common practice even today. Obviously, Polis would want to protect the canoe and see that it was kept safe and sound. But there are alternatives to what they did that should have been considered, at least by modern standards.

Reflect back on the various portages that they did: 2 two-milers, one ten-miler and numerous shorter ones. As a rule, the three travelers were strung out along each portage, often times separated completely from one another, struggling to get everything across the portage and often requiring two burdened carries which means 3 crossings. The latter fact is common and only on a trip where the travelers work like mules can they do it all in a single crossing.

Another common technique is for two people to carry the canoe, over their heads and on their shoulders, much as for a single person carry.

Now each person, if they are at least 15 to 17 years of age, can carry a pack as well as half the canoe weight. Polis should be one of the canoe and pack portagers, he could carry a pack weighing 35 to 45 pounds, and the weakest member should be his partner. In this case that should be the 'companion' because he always slowed down the carrying of the camp goods (his pack might be only 15 to 25 pounds in weight). Due to the particular circumstances, Joe should be in the front and he ought to be giving encouraging words to the 'companion.'

About five or ten paces behind them should be Henry carrying the rest of the goods as he demonstrated some real endurance and gusto in his work. Henry should also encourage his companion to keep on trucking and perhaps they all could sing songs as they moved along the portage. In this configuration a single pass might have been possible, but even if not, it keeps the group together and not getting anyone lost, it will be faster overall, and it deals with the comparative strength of each person while they all observe how Polis found his way and learn from him. This type of alteration, of course, is situational dependent and other trips might well be handled differently. It is up to the guide to observe and try different modalities. In fairness, no standards of guiding existed in 1857 and Joe in many ways (and other top native guides) was blazing a trail for others to improve upon.

15. July 31- East Branch

Polis was soon too weak to carry any burden; but he managed to catch one otter…

The Indian said, "You and I kill moose last night, therefore use 'em best wood. Always use hard wood to cook moose-meat." His "best wood" was rock maple. He cast the moose's lip into the fire, to burn the hair off, and then rolled it up with the meat to carry along. Observing that we were sitting down to breakfast without any pork, he said, with a very grave look, "Me want some fat," so he was told that he might have as much as he would fry.

We had smooth but swift water for a considerable distance, where we glided rapidly along, scaring up ducks and kingfishers. But, as usual, our smooth progress ere long came to an end, and we were obliged to carry canoe and all about half a mile down the right bank, around some rapids or falls. It required sharp eyes sometimes to tell which side was the carry, before you went over the falls, but Polis never failed to land us rightly. The raspberries were particularly abundant and large here, and all hands went to eating them, the Indian remarking on their size.

Often on bare rocky carries the trail was so

indistinct that I repeatedly lost it, but when I walked behind him I observed that he could keep it almost like a hound, and rarely hesitated, or, if he paused a moment on a bare rock, his eye immediately detected some sign which would have escaped me. Frequently we found no path at all at these places, and were to him unaccountably delayed. He would only say it was "ver strange."

We had heard of a Grand Fall on this stream, and thought that each fall we came to must be it, but after christening several in succession with this name, we gave up the search. There were more Grand or Petty Falls than I can remember.

I cannot tell how many times we had to walk on account of falls or rapids. We were expecting all the while that the river would take a final leap and get to smooth water, but there was no improvement this forenoon. However, the carries were an agreeable variety. So surely as we stepped out of the canoe and stretched our legs we found ourselves in a blueberry and raspberry garden, each side of our rocky trail around the falls being lined with one or both. There was not a carry on the main East Branch where we did not find an abundance of both these berries, for these were the rockiest places, and partially cleared, such as these plants prefer, and there had been none to gather the finest before us.

In our three journeys over the carries,—for we were obliged to go over the ground three times whenever the canoe was taken out,—we did full justice to the berries, and they were just what we wanted to correct the effect of our hard bread and pork diet. Another name for making a portage would have been going a-berrying. We also found a few *amelanchier*, or service, berries, though most were abortive, but they held on rather more generally than they do in Concord. The Indian called them pemoymenuk, and said that they bore much fruit in some places. He sometimes also ate the northern wild red cherries, saying that they were good medicine, but they were scarcely edible. We bathed and dined at the foot of one of these carries. It was the Indian who commonly reminded us that it was dinner-time, sometimes even by turning the prow to the shore. He once made an indirect, but lengthy apology, by saying that we might think it strange, but that one who worked hard all day was very particular to have his dinner in good season.

At the most considerable fall on this stream,

when I was walking over the carry, close behind the Indian, he observed a track on the rock, which was but slightly covered with soil, and, stooping, muttered "caribou." When we returned, he observed a much larger track near the same place, where some animal's foot had sunk into a small hollow in the rock, partly filled with grass and earth, and he exclaimed with surprise, "What that?" "Well, what is it?" I asked. Stooping and laying his hand in it, he answered with a mysterious air, and in a half whisper, "Devil [that is, Indian Devil, or cougar]—ledges about here—very bad animal—pull 'em rocks all to pieces." "How long since it was made?" I asked. "Today or yesterday," said he. But when I asked him afterward if he was sure it was the devil's track, he said he did not know. I had been told that the scream of a cougar was heard about Ktaadn recently, and we were not far from that mountain.

We spent at least half the time in walking today, and the walking was as bad as usual, for the Indian, being alone, commonly ran down far below the foot of the carries before he waited for us. The carry-paths themselves were more than usually indistinct, often the route being revealed only by the countless small holes in the fallen timber made by the tacks in the drivers' boots, or where there was a slight trail we did not find it. It was a tangled and perplexing thicket, through which we stumbled and threaded our way, and when we had finished a mile of it, our starting-point seemed far away. We were glad that we had not got to walk to Bangor along the banks of this river, which would be a journey of more than a hundred miles.

Think of the denseness of the forest, the fallen trees and rocks, the windings of the river, the streams emptying in, and the frequent swamps to be crossed. It made you shudder. Yet the Indian from time to time pointed out to us where he had thus crept along day after day when he was a boy of ten, and in a starving condition. He had been hunting far north of this with two grown Indians. The winter came on unexpectedly early, and the ice compelled them to leave their canoe at Grand Lake, and walk down the bank. They shouldered their furs and started for Oldtown. The snow was not deep enough for snowshoes, or to cover the inequalities of the ground. Polis was soon too weak to carry any burden; but he managed to catch one otter. This was the most they all had to eat on this journey, and he remembered how good the yellow lily roots were, made into a soup with the otter oil. He shared this food equally with the other two, but being so small he suffered much more than they. He waded through the Mattawamkeag at its mouth, when it was freezing cold and came up to his chin, and he, being very weak and emaciated, expected to be swept away. The first house which they reached was at Lincoln, and thereabouts they met a white teamster with supplies, who, seeing their condition, gave them as much of his load as they could eat. For six months after getting home, he was very low, and did not expect to live, and was perhaps always the worse for it.

We could not find much more than half of this day's journey on our maps (the "Map of the Public Lands of Maine and Massachusetts," and "Colton's Railroad and Township Map of Maine," which copies the former). By the maps there was not more than fifteen miles between camps at the outside, and yet we had been busily progressing all day, and much of the time very rapidly.

For seven or eight miles below that succession of "Grand" falls, the aspect of the banks as well as the character of the stream was changed.

After passing a tributary from the northeast, perhaps Bowlin Stream, we had good swift smooth water, with a regular slope, such as I have described. Low, grassy banks and muddy shores began. Many elms, as well as maples, and more ash trees, overhung the stream, and supplanted the spruce.

My lily roots having been lost when the canoe was taken out at a carry, I landed late in the afternoon, at a low and grassy place amid maples, to gather more. It was slow work, grubbing them up amid the sand, and the mosquitoes were all the while feasting on me. Mosquitoes, black flies, etc., pursued us in mid-channel, and we were glad sometimes to get into violent rapids, for then we escaped them.

A red-headed woodpecker flew across the river, and the Indian remarked that it was good to eat. As we glided swiftly down the inclined plane of the river, a great cat owl launched itself away from a stump on the bank, and flew heavily across the stream, and the Indian, as usual, imitated its note. Soon the same bird flew back in front of us, and we afterwards passed it perched on a tree. Soon afterward a white-headed eagle sailed down the stream before us. We drove him several miles, while we were looking for a good place to camp, for we expected to be overtaken by a shower,—and still we could distinguish him by his white tail, sailing away from time to time from some tree by the shore still farther down the stream. Some shecorways being surprised by us, a part of them dived, and we passed directly over them, and could trace their course here and there by a bubble on the surface, but we did not see them come up. Polis detected once or twice what he called a "tow" road, an indistinct path leading into the forest. In the meanwhile we passed the mouth of the Seboois on our left. This did not look so large as our stream, which was indeed the main one. It was some time before we found a camping-place, for the shore was either too grassy and muddy, where mosquitoes abounded, or too steep a hillside. The Indian said that there were but few mosquitoes on a steep hillside. We examined a good place, where somebody had camped a long time; but it seemed pitiful to occupy an old site, where there was so much room to choose, so we continued on. We at length found a place to our minds, on the west bank, about a mile below the mouth of the Seboois, where, in a very dense spruce wood above a gravelly shore, there seemed to be but few insects. The trees were so thick that we were obliged to clear a space to build our fire and lie down in, and the young spruce trees that were left were like the wall of an apartment rising around us. We were obliged to pull ourselves up a steep bank to get there. But the place which you have selected for your camp, though never so rough and grim, begins at once to have its attractions, and becomes a very centre of civilization to you: "Home is home, be it never so homely."

It turned out that the mosquitoes were more numerous here than we had found them before, and the Indian complained a good deal, though he lay, as the night before, between three fires and his stretched hide. As I sat on a stump by the fire, with a veil and gloves on, trying to read, he observed, "I make you candle," and in a minute he took a piece of birch bark about two inches wide and rolled it hard, like an allumette fifteen inches long, lit it, and fixed it by the other end horizontally in a split stick three feet high, stuck it in the ground, turning the blazing end to the wind, and telling me to snuff it from time to time. It answered the purpose of a candle pretty well.

I noticed, as I had done before, that there was a lull among the mosquitoes about midnight, and that they began again in the morning. Nature is thus merciful. But apparently they need rest as well as we. Few, if any, creatures are equally active all night. As soon as it was light I saw, through my veil, that the inside of the tent about our heads was quite blackened with myriads, each one of their wings when flying, as has been calculated,

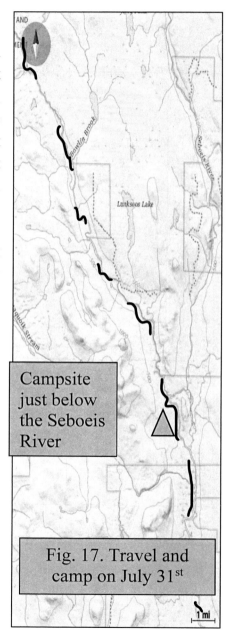

Campsite just below the Seboeis River

Fig. 17. Travel and camp on July 31st

vibrating some three thousand times in a minute, and their combined hum was almost as bad to endure as their stings. I had an uncomfortable night on this account though I am not sure that one succeeded in his attempt to sting me. We did not suffer so much from insects on this excursion as the statements of some who have explored these woods in midsummer led us to anticipate. Yet I have no doubt that at some seasons and in some places they are a much more serious pest. The Jesuit Hierome Lalemant, of Quebec, reporting the death of Father Reni Menard, who was abandoned, lost his way, and died in the woods, among the Ontarios near Lake Superior, in 1661, dwells chiefly on his probable sufferings from the attacks of mosquitoes when too weak to defend himself, adding that there was a frightful number of them in those parts, "and so insupportable," says he, "that the three Frenchmen who have made that voyage affirm that there was no other means of defending one's self but to run always without stopping, and it was even necessary for two of them to be employed in driving off these creatures while the third wanted to drink, otherwise he could not have done it." I have no doubt that this was said in good faith.

Comment:

This day's entry holds little new for the trip taken as a whole, but several insights are still to be found. Joe Polis' experiences as a 10-year-old are stunning and surely portended a life of great strength and resourcefulness. How he could 'catch' an otter and then make a soup is hard to fathom. The generosity of the white teamster, feeding the three of them abundantly, may have left Joe with a positive outlook to white settlers and visitors.

The discussion about mosquitoes is not an exaggeration at all and is still common in many parts of the US and Canada today. Needing a person to shoo flies away as one is drinking is clear; but what about the more complex task of relieving oneself in the wild? Unspeakable!

16. August 1- Smooth Waters

… he took refuge under the tent with us, and gave us a song before falling asleep.

I caught two or three large red chivin (*Leuciscus pulchellus*) early this morning, within twenty feet of the camp, which, added to the moose-tongue, that had been left in the kettle boiling overnight, and to our other stores, made a sumptuous breakfast. The Indian made us some hemlock tea instead of coffee, and we were not obliged to go as far as China for it; indeed, not quite so far as for the fish. This was tolerable, though he said it was not strong enough. It was interesting to see so simple a dish as a kettle of water with a handful of green hemlock sprigs in it, boiling over the huge fire in the open air, the leaves fast losing their lively green color, and know that it was for our breakfast.

We were glad to embark once more, and leave some of the mosquitoes behind. We had passed the Wassataquoik without perceiving it. This, according to the Indian, is the name of the main East Branch itself, and not properly applied to this small tributary alone, as on the maps. We found that we had camped about a mile above Hunt's, which is on the east bank, and is the last house for those who ascend Ktaadn on this side.

We had expected to ascend it from this point, but my companion was obliged to give up this on account of sore feet. The Indian, however, suggested that perhaps he might get a pair of moccasins at this place, and that he could walk very easily in them without hurting his feet, wearing several pairs of stockings, and he said beside that they were so porous that when you had taken in water it all drained out again in a little while. We stopped to get some sugar, but found that the family had moved away, and the house was unoccupied, except temporarily by some men who were getting the hay. They told me that the road to Ktaadn left the river eight miles above; also that perhaps we could get some sugar at Fisk's, fourteen miles below. I do not remember that we saw the mountain at all from the river. I noticed a seine here stretched on the bank, which probably had been used to catch salmon. Just below this, on the west bank, we saw a moose-hide stretched, and with it a bearskin, which was comparatively very small. I was the more interested in this sight, because it was near here that a townsman of ours, then quite a lad, and alone, killed a large bear some years ago. The Indian said that they belonged to

Joe Aitteon, my last guide, but how he told I do not know. He was probably hunting near, and had left them for the day. Finding that we were going directly to Oldtown, he regretted that he had not taken more of the moose-meat to his family, saying that in a short time, by drying it, he could have made it so light as to have brought away the greater part, leaving the bones. We once or twice inquired after the lip, which is a famous tidbit, but he said, "That go Oldtown for my old woman; don't get it every day."

Maples grew more and more numerous. It was lowering, and rained a little during the forenoon, and, as we expected a wetting, we stopped early and dined on the east side of a small expansion of the river, just above what are probably called Whetstone Falls, about a dozen miles below Hunt's. There were pretty fresh moose-tracks by the waterside. There were singular long ridges hereabouts, called "horsebacks," covered with ferns. My companion, having lost his pipe, asked the Indian if he could not make him one. "Oh, yer," said he, and in a minute rolled up one of birch bark, telling him to wet the bowl from time to time. Here also he left his Gazette on a tree.

We carried round the falls just

below, on the west side. The rocks were on their edges, and very sharp. The distance was about three fourths of a mile. When we had carried over one load, the Indian returned by the shore, and I by the path, and though I made no particular haste, I was nevertheless surprised to find him at the other end as soon as I. It was remarkable how easily he got along over the worst ground. He said to me, "I take canoe and you take the rest, suppose you can keep along with me?" I thought that he meant that while he ran down the rapids I should keep along the shore, and be ready to assist him from time to time, as I had done before; but as the walking would be very bad, I answered, "I suppose you will go too fast for me, but I will try." But I was to go by the path, he said. This I thought would not help the matter, I should have so far to go to get to the riverside when he wanted me. But neither was this what he meant. He was proposing a race over the carry, and asked me if I thought I could keep along with him by the same path, adding that I must be pretty smart to do it. As his load, the canoe, would be much the heaviest and bulkiest, though the simplest, I thought that I ought to be able to do it, and said that I would try. So I proceeded to gather up the gun, axe, paddle, kettle, frying-pan, plates, dippers, carpets, etc., etc., and while I was thus engaged he threw me his cowhide boots. "What, are these in the bargain?" I asked. "Oh, yer," said he; but before I could make a bundle of my load I saw him disappearing over a hill with the canoe on his head; so, hastily scraping the various articles together, I started on the run, and immediately went by him in the bushes, but I had no sooner left him out of sight in a rocky hollow than the greasy plates, dippers, etc., took to themselves wings, and while I was employed in gathering them up again, he went by me; but hastily pressing the sooty kettle to my side, I started once more, and soon passing him again, I saw him no more on the carry. I do not mention this as anything of a feat, for it was but poor running on my part, and he was obliged to move with great caution for fear of breaking his canoe as well as his neck. When he made his appearance, puffing and panting like myself, in answer to my inquiries where he had been, he said, "Rocks (locks) cut 'em feet," and, laughing, added, "Oh, me love to play sometimes." He said that he and his companions, when they came to carries several miles long, used to try who would get over first; each, perhaps, with a canoe on his head. I bore the sign of the kettle on my brown linen sack for the rest of the voyage.

We made a second carry on the west side, around some falls about a mile below this. On the mainland were Norway pines, indicating a new geological formation, and it was such a dry and sandy soil as we had not noticed before.

As we approached the mouth of the East Branch, we passed two or three huts, the first sign of civilization after Hunt's, though we saw no road as yet; we heard a cow-bell, and even saw an infant held up to a small square window to see us pass, but apparently the infant and the mother that held it were the only inhabitants then at home for several miles. This took the wind out of our sails, reminding us that we were travelers surely, while it was a native of the soil, and had the advantage of us. Conversation flagged. I would only hear the Indian, perhaps, ask my companion, "You load my pipe?" He said that he smoked alder bark, for medicine. On entering the West Branch at Nicketow it appeared much larger than the East. Polis remarked that the former was all gone and lost now, that it was all smooth water hence to Oldtown, and he threw away his pole which was cut on the

Umbazookskus. Thinking of the rapids, he said once or twice that you wouldn't catch him to go East Branch again; but he did not by any means mean all that he said.

Things are quite changed since I was here eleven years ago. Where there were but one or two houses, I now found quite a village, with sawmills and a store (the latter was locked, but its contents were so much the more safely stored), and there was a stage-road to Mattawamkeag, and the rumor of a stage. Indeed, a steamer had ascended thus far once, when the water was very high. But we were not able to get any sugar, only a better shingle to lean our backs against.

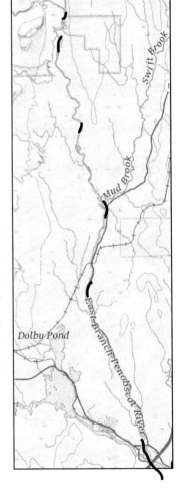

Fig. 18. Travel on Aug. 1st

We camped about two miles below Nicketow, on the south side of the West Branch, covering with fresh twigs the withered bed of a former traveler, and feeling that we were now in a settled country, especially when in the evening we heard an ox sneeze in its wild pasture across the river. Wherever you land along the frequented part of the river, you have not far to go to find these sites of temporary inns, the withered bed of flattened twigs, the charred sticks, and perhaps the tent-poles. And not long since, similar beds were spread along the Connecticut, the Hudson, and the Delaware, and longer still ago, by the Thames and Seine, and they now help to make the soil where private and public gardens, mansions and palaces are. We could not get fir twigs for our bed here, and the spruce was harsh in comparison, having more twig in proportion to its leaf, but we improved it somewhat with hemlock. The Indian remarked as before, "Must have hard wood to cook moose-meat," as if that were a maxim, and proceeded to get it. My companion cooked some in California fashion, winding a long string of the meat round a stick and slowly turning it in his hand before the fire. It was very good. But the Indian, not approving of the mode, or because he was not allowed to cook it his own way, would not taste it. After the regular supper we attempted to make a lily soup of the bulbs which I had brought along, for I wished to learn all I could before I got out of the woods. Following the Indian's directions, for he began to be sick, I washed the bulbs carefully, minced some moose-meat and some pork, salted and boiled all together, but we had not patience to try the experiment fairly,

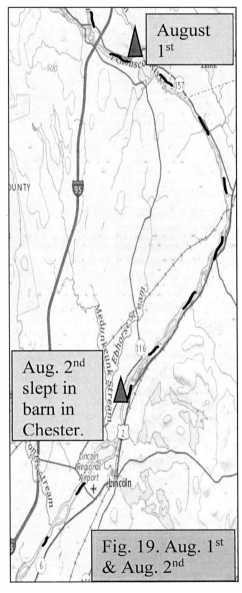

August 1st

Aug. 2nd slept in barn in Chester.

Fig. 19. Aug. 1st & Aug. 2nd

for he said it must be boiled till the roots were completely softened so as to thicken the soup like flour; but though we left it on all night, we found it dried to the kettle in the morning, and not yet boiled to a flour. Perhaps the roots were not ripe enough, for they commonly gather them in the fall. As it was, it was palatable enough, but it reminded me of the Irishman's limestone broth. The other ingredients were enough alone. The Indian's name for these bulbs was Sheepnoc. I stirred the soup by accident with a striped maple or moose-wood stick, which I had peeled, and he remarked that its bark was an emetic.

He prepared to camp as usual between his moose-hide and the fire; but it beginning to rain suddenly, he took refuge under the tent with us, and gave us a song before falling asleep. It rained hard in the night, and spoiled another box of matches for us, which the Indian had left out, for he was very careless; but, as usual, we had so much the better night for the rain, since it kept the mosquitoes down.

Comments:

A little fun competition began, of Joe's origin, and played out rather well:

> *...while I was employed in gathering them up again, he went by me; but hastily pressing the sooty kettle to my side, I started once more, and soon passing him again, I saw him no more on the carry. I do not mention this as anything of a feat, for it was but poor running on my part, and he was obliged to move with great caution for fear of breaking his canoe as well as his neck. When he made his appearance, puffing and panting like myself, in answer to my inquiries where he had been, he said, "Rocks (locks) cut 'em feet," and, laughing, added, "Oh, me love to play sometimes."*

Truly a highpoint when the two of them relax enough to get into a playful race; a much better relationship then the frigid start to the trip when Polis sat stoically and wordlessly on the coach out of Bangor. As a guide, I would never agree to a race of this type as the slips and falls can be painful if not debilitating. I well know as I have a compression fractured vertebrae from a similar canoe-portage slip and fall.

17. *Vignette 5*: Communication

Good communication skills are essential for any success and effective purpose in life. Suppose we go for a day canoe trip together down a river with class 1 or 2 rapids. This would be your first canoe trip but not for me and I have been down the selected river before and am reasonably sure of the details, subject to the weather. I have taken about an hour before starting the trip to review the strokes that you will need in the bow, what I will be doing in the stern, how we will communicate, and safety procedures covering several matters including capsizing in rapids, which of course should not ever happen in class 1 or 2 rapids unless a bizarre event occurred. And we practice this before starting.

So off you and I go on our day paddle, and all goes well. I point out at the beginning that the water level is perfect for the trip and we move along very nicely. Good scenery, sunny, nice temperatures just a pleasant drift and paddling downstream. I notice, however, that the water level for the stream is no longer as full possibly due to some lack of rain; at the start of our trip the river was fed by an upstream large lake but downstream where the stream widens a lot, the stream should add volumes of water from side streams but these were lacking rain water at this time. Still, the river was very navigable and caused no alarm. Near the end, however, the rapids appeared but now they were perhaps Class 3 and you found them to be frightening.

Fig 20. West Branch Penobscot beauty

I took a close look at the full stream width and chose a good path through the rapids. We started in and worked around the first few rocks and then fast water came upon us and fast turns were needed so as to not broach the canoe against these rocks. As we had trained, I called out the needed stroke: "draw right" I called out seemingly followed by little reaction from you. We were closing fast on a large obstacle with little reaction from the bow while I was furiously sweeping hard in the stern. "draw right…draw *right …draw right hard NOW!*" My voice rose as we neared the boulder and then all clicked together and we started to pass the large rock safely, only scraping on the port side and potentially hanging up a bit, but not so, as I leaned forward, placing my left foot against the rock and shoved on downstream. And we made it through very nicely.

But how did you feel about that encounter and a nearly failed communication effort? Relieved of course, but angry that we got into that stream, annoyed at my rising voice, and ready to quit? Or, were you pleased that we handled a tricky unexpected challenge quite well? Would we be able to talk about this and iron out any residual feelings?

(Incidentally, this introduction is only slightly modified from a real experience in the year of this writing with my wife in our canoe on the very same river, the West Branch of the Penobscot, 164 years after the Thoreau-Polis trip passed through on the very same week of the year. The rapids were just before where the Pine stream joins in and where Polis paddled, even though he tells of two men who died there several years before. The river is different today due to increased height of the dams and it is commonly used for safe day trips by local outfitters and guides.)

Now, as we get back to the Thoreau-Polis story, let us think about how these strangers handled many similar events. Did they become fast friends, did they respect each other, did they grow with the experiences, and did they really understand each other?

On the very first day of meeting and working together Joe and Henry had this experience:

> I tried to enter into conversation with him, but as he was puffing under the weight of his canoe, not having the usual apparatus for carrying it, but, above all, was an Indian, I might as well have been thumping on the bottom of his birch the while. In answer to the various observations which I made by way of breaking the ice, he only grunted vaguely from beneath his canoe once or twice, so that I knew he was there.

Soon they began some of the usual ritual of getting a handle on who each person was and how to address them:

> He never addressed us by our names, though curious to know how they were spelled and what they meant, while we called him Polis. He had already guessed very accurately at our ages, and said that he was forty-eight.

And riding for a day from Bangor to Greenville

amidst the rain and closed up in a stagecoach or at an inn for a break or lunch we can note:

> The Indian sat on the front seat, saying nothing to anybody, with a stolid expression of face, as if barely awake to what was going on. Again I was struck by the peculiar vagueness of his replies when addressed in the stage, or at the taverns. He really never said anything on such occasions. He was merely stirred up, like a wild beast, and passively muttered some insignificant response. His answer, in such cases, was never the consequence of a positive mental energy, but vague as a puff of smoke, suggesting no responsibility, and if you considered it, you would find that you had got nothing out of him. This was instead of the conventional palaver and smartness of the white man, and equally profitable. Most get no more than this out of the Indian, and pronounce him stolid accordingly. I was surprised to see what a foolish and impertinent style a Maine man, a passenger, used in addressing him, as if he were a child, which only made his eyes glisten a little. A tipsy Canadian asked him at a tavern, in a drawling tone, if he smoked, to which he answered with an indefinite "Yes." "Won't you lend me your pipe a little while?" asked the other. He replied, looking straight by the man's head, with a face singularly vacant to all neighboring interests, "Me got no pipe;" yet I had seen him put a new one, with a supply of tobacco, into his pocket that morning."

Even these first two days are telling. Trying to start a conversation with anyone laboring under a 80-pound canoe on a circa ¾ mile portage through a city is quite daft. Thoreau could have tried to imagine what such a portage would be like and just bide his time. Of course he got no reply! Soon Joe Polis started a conversation about their respective ages; what a wonderful time that might have been to also talk about names and what each person was accustomed to or what each person preferred to be called. They did fall into a name pattern that worked but missed a chance to understand each other better. Why Henry kept referring to Joe as "the Indian," at least in his writing, is unclear and insensitive in modern times but perhaps not then. Referring to anyone as 'the this or that' is lazy and likely insensitive, though if he used it out loud it seems that Joe took no offense, to his credit. Thoreau says that they called him "Polis" but he used that name for reference rarely in his writing.

The stagecoach discourses speak for themselves – Joe was derided more than once and he just sank into his own private world for the day. Thoreau's words and phrases were not well chosen and he would probably regret what he had written if he could have seen the final manuscript before publishing but, unfortunately, he was already dead. Joe, to his credit, seemed to spring back quickly the next day when in his canoe and the voyage was under way.

Developing a mutual teaching and learning cycle between two people takes patience, tolerance, and forgiveness as either one may overstep human behavioral boundaries. Intelligence, humor, and wit are also very helpful. It is easy to be offended when giving direct response to each other. Here are six examples from Thoreau's text:

In this first case, Thoreau messed with the local ecology rather than using a proper grease pit for disposal. Joe admonishes him by pointing out the consequences (a sluggish canoe ride) but tempers the comment by adding 'So says old times.'

> After breakfast I, Henry, emptied the melted pork that was left into the lake, making what sailors call a "slick," and watching to see how much it spread over and smoothed the agitated surface. The Indian looked at it a moment and said, "That make hard paddlum thro'; hold 'em canoe. So say old times."

In the second case, Thoreau makes a very thoughtful request, actually two requests, and they were well acknowledged and the last one was agreed to.

> I observed that I should like to go to school to him to learn his language, living on the Indian island the while; could not that be done? "Oh, yer," he replied, "good many do so." I asked how long he thought it would take. He said one week. I told him that in this voyage I would tell him all I knew, and he should tell me all he knew, to which he readily agreed.

The third case got very sensitive as it dealt with religion, which each man discussed rather openly. Somewhat out of character Joe tells Thoreau point-blank that his habits are '...ver bad' but Thoreau's companion evidently sided with Joe on this matter and at this moment Thoreau took it rather well.

> [Joe] asked me how I spent the Sunday when at home. I told him that I commonly sat in my chamber reading, etc., in the forenoon, and went to walk in the afternoon. At which he shook his head and said, "Er, that is ver bad." "How do you spend it?" I asked. He said that he did no work, that he went to church at Oldtown when he was at home; in short, he did as he had been taught by the whites. This led to a discussion in which I found myself in the minority.

One must question the assertion that 'he did as he had been taught by the whites.' Is that Thoreau's notion or did Joe say it? Did Joe adopt his practice upon joining the church or did he come to his preference over time and under many influences? Then Joe goes on to find a way forward but later Thoreau holds him accountable for not following his strategy.

> However, the Indian added, plying the paddle all the while, that if we would go along, he must go with us, he our man, and he suppose that if he no takum pay for what he do Sunday, then ther's no harm, but if he takum pay, then wrong. I told him that he was stricter than white men. Nevertheless, I noticed that he did not forget to reckon in the Sundays at last.

> He appeared to be a very religious man, and said his prayers in a loud voice, in Indian, kneeling before the camp, morning and evening,—sometimes scrambling up again in haste when he had forgotten this, and saying them with great rapidity.

A useful question is which of the two, Joe with commendable Christian practices and rote recitations or Thoreau with his transcendent view of everything around him, best enjoyed a good life and had a positive influence on those around him?

In the quote below, Joe's commentary on the whites would be readily accepted by many today.

> He criticised the people of the United States as compared with other nations, but the only distinct idea with which he labored was, that they were "very strong," but, like some individuals, "too fast."

He must have the credit of saying this just before the general breaking down of railroads and banks. He had a great idea of education, and would occasionally break out into such expressions as this, "Kademy—a-cad-e-my—good thing—I suppose they usum Fifth Reader there You been college?

Changing focus, Thoreau ponders the fact of getting lost while Joe shows restraint yet still expressing his surprise over their lack of skill. In the third paragraph, Thoreau triumphs, presumably with his map and compass skills but also does not rub it in and showed restraint.

After a long while my companion came back, and the Indian with him. We had taken the wrong road, and the Indian had lost us. He had very wisely gone back to the Canadian's camp, and asked him which way we had probably gone, since he could better understand the ways of white men, and he told him correctly that we had undoubtedly taken the supply road to Chamberlain Lake (slender supplies they would get over such a road at this season). The Indian was greatly surprised that we should have taken what he called a "tow" (i. e., tote or toting or supply) road, instead of a carry path,—that we had not followed his tracks,—said it was "strange," and evidently thought little of our woodcraft.

Frequently we found no path at all at these places, and were to him unaccountably delayed. He would only say it was 'ver strange.'

It was not apparent where the outlet of this lake was,

and while the Indian thought it was in one direction, I thought it was in another. He said, "I bet you fourpence it is there," but he still held on in my direction, which proved to be the right one.

Here, below, Thoreau applauds Joe's superior manners and learns Joe's means of nudging them in a good direction without making a big fuss over the issues. Joe was polite and restrained throughout except when he told Thoreau that it was not good to stay in his study instead of going to church.

He seemed to be very saving of his breath,—yet he would be surprised if we went by, or did not strike the right spot. This was not because he was unaccommodating, but a proof of superior manners. Indians like to get along with the least possible communication and ado. He was really paying us a great compliment all the while, thinking that we preferred a hint to a kick.

It is commendable that Thoreau saw the light side of Joe coming out in the evening; of course, Joe was a paid guide and surely felt a lot of responsibilities during the day.

Especially after the day's work was over, and he had put himself in posture for the night, he would be unexpectedly sociable, exhibit even the bonhommie of a Frenchman, and we would fall asleep before he got through his periods.

Credit here goes to Thoreau for stepping away from earlier pejorative language (savages) and found respect for commendable social graces.

> The Penobscot Indians seem to be more social, even, than the whites. Ever and anon in the deepest wilderness of Maine, you come to the log hut of a Yankee or Canada settler, but a Penobscot never takes up his residence in such a solitude. They are not even scattered about on their islands in the Penobscot, which are all within the settlements, but gathered together on two or three,— though not always on the best soil,—evidently for the sake of society.

> Polis had evidently more curiosity respecting the few settlers in those woods than we. If nothing was said, he took it for granted that we wanted to go straight to the next log-hut. Having observed that we came by the log huts at Chesuncook, and the blind Canadian's at the Mud Pond carry, without stopping to communicate with the inhabitants, he took occasion now to suggest that the usual way was, when you came near a house, to go to it, and tell the inhabitants what you had seen or heard, and then they tell you what they had seen; but we laughed, and said that we had had enough of houses for the present, and had come here partly to avoid them.

The following event reflects a stoicism in Joe that often is not seen. At about age 18, I took a very similar fall and it hurt very badly. It took several minutes before I could reposition my canoe and continue the portage; this might have been the event in my life that crushed a vertebra in my spine.

> In going over this portage the last time, the Indian, who was before me with the canoe on his head, stumbled and fell heavily once, and lay for a moment silent, as if in pain. I hastily stepped forward to help him, asking if he was much hurt, but after a moment's pause, without replying, he sprang up and went forward. He was all the way subject to taciturn fits, but they were harmless ones.

We also see a very Euro-American response to a sudden joyful event but not a response that Joe would use. Again, a part of his stoicism but also an understanding that it is best in the woods not to make much noise unless scaring a bear or moose away.

> I heard an answering shout from my companion, and soon after saw him standing on a point where there was a clearing a quarter of a mile below, and the smoke of his fire was rising nearby. Before I saw him I naturally shouted again and again, but the Indian curtly remarked, "He hears you," as if once was enough.

The question of effective communication continues with the last two days of the trip, as follows now. But we can first return to the original questions from the start of this chapter: 'let us think about how these strangers handled many similar events. Did they become fast friends, did they respect each other, did they grow with the experiences, and did they really understand each other?'

18. August 2- How to Talk

May be your way talking, may be all right, no Indian way.

Me doctor,—first study my case, find out what ail 'em,—
then I know what to take.

Sunday was a cloudy and unpromising morning. One of us observed to the Indian, "You did not stretch your moose-hide last night, did you, Mr. Polis?" Whereat he replied, in a tone of surprise, though perhaps not of ill humor: "What you ask me that question for? Suppose I stretch 'em, you see 'em. May be your way talking, may be all right, no Indian way." I had observed that he did not wish to answer the same question more than once, and was often silent when it was put again for the sake of certainty, as if he were moody. Not that he was incommunicative, for he frequently commenced a long-winded narrative of his own accord,—repeated at length the tradition of some old battle, or some passage in the recent history of his tribe in which he had acted a prominent part, from time to time drawing a long breath, and resuming the thread of his tale, with the true story-teller's leisureliness, perhaps after shooting a rapid,— prefacing with "We-e-ll, by-by," etc., as he paddled along. Especially after the day's work was over, and he had put himself in posture for the night, he would be unexpectedly sociable, exhibit even the bonhommie of a Frenchman, and we would fall asleep before he got through his periods.

Nicketow is called eleven miles from Mattawamkeag by the river. Our camp was, therefore, about nine miles from the latter place.

The Indian was quite sick this morning with the colic. I thought that he was the worse for the moose-meat he had eaten.

We reached the Mattawamkeag at half past eight in the morning, in the midst of a drizzling rain, and, after buying some sugar, set out again.

The Indian growing much worse, we stopped in the north part of Lincoln to get some brandy for him; but failing in this, an apothecary recommended Brandreth's pills, which he refused to take, because he was not acquainted with them. He said to me, "Me doctor,—first study my case, find out what ail 'em,—then I know what to take." We dropped down a little farther, and stopped at mid-forenoon on an island and made him a dipper of tea. Here, too, we dined and did some washing and botanizing, while he lay on the bank. In the afternoon we went on a little farther, though the Indian was no better. "Burntibus," as he called it, was a long, smooth, lake-like reach below the Five Islands. He said that he owned a hundred acres somewhere up this way. As a thunder-shower appeared to be coming up, we stopped opposite a barn on the west bank, in Chester, about a mile above Lincoln. Here at last we were obliged to spend the rest of the day and night, on account of our patient, whose sickness did not abate. He lay groaning under his canoe on the bank, looking very woebegone, yet it was only a common case of colic. You would not have thought, if you had seen him lying about thus, that he was the proprietor of so many acres in that neighborhood, was worth six thousand dollars, and had been to Washington. It seemed to me that, like the Irish, he made a greater ado about his sickness than a Yankee does, and was more alarmed about himself. We talked somewhat of leaving him with his people in Lincoln,—for that is one of their homes,—and taking the stage the next day, but he objected on account of the expense saying, "Suppose me well in morning, you and I go Oldtown by noon."

As we were taking our tea at twilight, while he lay groaning still under his canoe, having at length found out "what ail him," he asked me to get him a dipper of water. Taking the dipper in one hand he seized his powder-horn with the other, and, pouring into it a charge or two of powder, stirred it up with his finger, and drank it off. This was all he took today after breakfast beside his tea.

To save the trouble of pitching our tent, when we had secured our stores from wandering dogs, we camped in the solitary half-open barn near the bank, with the permission of the owner, lying on new-mown hay four feet deep. The fragrance of the hay, in which many ferns, etc., were mingled, was agreeable, though it was quite alive with grasshoppers which you could hear crawling through it. This served to graduate our approach to houses and feather beds. In the night some large bird, probably an owl, flitted through over our heads, and very early in the morning we were awakened by the twittering of swallows which had their nests there.

Comments:

Discovering the real Joe Polis requires a thorough reading of Thoreau's writing and looking for the slightest clues…

he was the proprietor of so many acres in that neighborhood, was worth six thousand dollars, and had been to Washington.

Just a tidbit of curious information on Joe Polis, creeping out at the strangest moments.

Chapter 19. August 3, Last Train Home

It makes no difference to me where I am.

This was the last that I saw of Joe Polis. We took the last train, and reached Bangor that night.

We started early before breakfast, the Indian being considerably better, and soon glided by Lincoln, and after another long and handsome lake-like reach, we stopped to breakfast on the west shore, two or three miles below this town.

We frequently passed Indian islands with their small houses on them. The Governor, Aitteon, lives in one of them, in Lincoln.

The Penobscot Indians seem to be more social, even, than the whites. Ever and anon in the deepest wilderness of Maine, you come to the log hut of a Yankee or Canada settler, but a Penobscot never takes up his residence in such a solitude. They are not even scattered about on their islands in the Penobscot, which are all within the settlements, but gathered together on two or three,— though not always on the best soil,—evidently for the sake of society. I saw one or two houses not now used by them, because, as our Indian Polis said, they were too solitary.

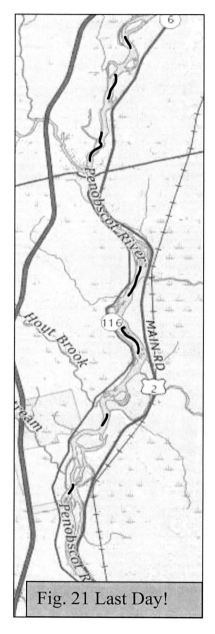

Fig. 21 Last Day!

The small river emptying in at Lincoln is the Matanancook, which also, we noticed, was the name of a steamer moored there. So we paddled and floated along, looking into the mouths of rivers. When passing the Mohawk Rips, or, as the Indian called them, "Mohog lips," four or five miles below Lincoln, he told us at length the story of a fight between his tribe and the Mohawks there, anciently,— how the latter were overcome by stratagem, the Penobscots using concealed knives,—

but they could not for a long time kill the Mohawk chief, who was a very large and strong man, though he was attacked by several canoes at once, when swimming alone in the river.

From time to time we met Indians in their canoes, going up river. Our man did not commonly approach them, but exchanged a few words with them at a distance in his tongue. These were the first Indians we had met since leaving the Umbazookskus.

At Piscataquis Falls, just above the river of that name, we walked over the wooden railroad on the eastern shore, about one and a half miles long, while the Indian glided down the rapids. The steamer from Oldtown stops here, and passengers take a new boat above. Piscataquis, whose mouth we here passed, means "branch." It is obstructed by falls at its mouth, but can be navigated with batteaux or canoes above through a settled country, even to the neighborhood of Moosehead Lake, and we had thought at first of going that way. We were not obliged to get out of the canoe after this on account of falls or rapids, nor, indeed, was it quite necessary here. We took less notice of the scenery to-day, because we were in quite a settled country. The river became broad and sluggish, and we saw a blue heron winging its way slowly down the stream before us.

We passed the Passadumkeag River on our left and saw the blue Olamon mountains at a distance in the southeast. Hereabouts our Indian told us at length the story of their contention with the priest respecting schools. He thought a great deal of education and had recommended it to his tribe. His argument in its favor was, that if you had been to college and learnt to calculate, you could "keep 'em property,—no other way." He said that his boy was the best scholar in the school at Oldtown, to which he went with whites. He himself is a Protestant, and goes to church regularly at Oldtown. According to his account, a good many of his tribe are Protestants, and many of the Catholics also are in favor of schools. Some years ago they had a schoolmaster, a Protestant, whom they liked very well. The priest came and said that they must send him away, and finally he had such influence, telling them that they would go to the bad place at last if they retained him, that they sent him away. The school party, though numerous, were about giving up. Bishop Fenwick came from Boston and used his influence against them. But our Indian told his side that they must not give up, must hold on, they were the strongest. If they gave up, then they would have no party. But they answered that it was "no use, priest too strong, we'd better give up." At length he persuaded them to make a stand.

The priest was going for a saw to cut down the liberty-pole. So Polis and his party had a secret meeting about it; he got ready fifteen or twenty stout young men, "stript 'em naked, and painted 'em like old times," and told them that when the priest and his party went to cut down the liberty-pole, they were to rush up, take hold of it, and prevent them, and he assured them that there would be no war, only a noise,—"no war where priest is." He kept his men concealed in a house near by, and when the priest's party were about to cut down the liberty-pole, the fall of which would have been a death-blow to the school party, he gave a signal, and his young men rushed out and seized the pole. There was a great uproar, and they were about coming to blows, but the priest interfered, saying, "No war, no war," and so the pole stands, and the school goes on still.

We thought that it showed a good deal of tact in him, to seize this occasion and take his stand on it; proving how well he understood those with whom he had to deal.

The Olamon River comes in from the east in Greenbush a few miles below the Passadumkeag. When we asked the meaning of this name, the Indian said there was an island opposite its mouth which was called Olarmon; that in old times, when visitors were coming to Oldtown, they used to stop there to dress and fix up or paint themselves. "What is that which ladies used?" he asked. Rouge? Red Vermilion? "Yer," he said, "that is larmon, a kind of clay or red paint, which they used to get here."

We decided that we, too, would stop at this island, and fix up our inner man, at least, by dining.

It was a large island, with an abundance of hemp nettle, but I did not notice any kind of red paint there. The Olamon River, at its mouth at least, is a dead stream. There was another large island in that neighborhood, which the Indian called "Soogle" (i. e., Sugar) Island.

About a dozen miles before reaching Oldtown he inquired, "How you like 'em your pilot?" But we postponed an answer till we had got quite back again.

The Sunkhaze, another short dead stream, comes in from the east two miles above Oldtown. There is said to be some of the best deer ground in Maine on this stream. Asking the meaning of this name, the Indian said, "Suppose you are going down Penobscot, just like we, and you see a canoe come out of bank and go along before you, but you no see 'em stream. That is Sunkhaze."

He had previously complimented me on my paddling, saying that I paddled "just like anybody," giving me an Indian name which meant "great paddler." When off this stream he said to me, who sat in the bows, "Me teach you paddle." So, turning toward the shore, he got out, came forward, and placed my hands as he wished. He placed one of them quite outside the boat, and the other parallel with the first, grasping the paddle near the end, not over the flat extremity, and told me to slide it back and forth on the side of the canoe. This, I found, was a great improvement which I had not thought of, saving me the labor of lifting the paddle each time, and I wondered that he had not suggested it before. It is true, before our baggage was reduced we had been obliged to sit with our legs drawn up, and our knees above the side of the canoe, which would have prevented our paddling thus, or perhaps he was afraid of wearing out his canoe, by constant friction on the side.

I told him that I had been accustomed to sit in the stern, and, lifting my paddle at each stroke, give it a twist in order to steer the boat, only getting a pry on the side each time, and I still paddled partly as if in the stern. He then wanted to see me paddle in the stern. So, changing paddles, for he had the longer and better one, and turning end for end, he sitting flat on the bottom and I on the crossbar, he began to paddle very hard, trying to turn the canoe, looking over his shoulder and laughing; but finding it in vain, he relaxed his efforts, though we still sped along a mile or two very swiftly. He said that he had no fault to find with my paddling in the stern, but I complained that he did not paddle according to his own directions in the bows.

Opposite the Sunkhaze is the main boom of the Penobscot, where the logs from far up the river are collected and assorted.

As we drew near to Oldtown I asked Polis if he was not glad to get home again; but there was no relenting to his wildness, and he said, "It makes no difference to me where I am." Such is the Indian's pretense always.

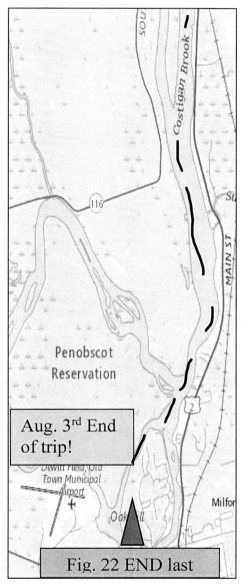

Aug. 3rd End of trip!

Fig. 22 END last

We approached the Indian Island through the narrow strait called "Cook." He said, "I 'xpect we take in some water there, river so high,—never see it so high at this season. Very rough water there, but short; swamp steamboat once. Don't you paddle till I tell you, then you paddle right along." It was a very short rapid. When we were in the midst of it he shouted "paddle," and we shot through without taking in a drop.

Soon after the Indian houses came in sight, but I could not at first tell my companion which of two or three large white ones was our guide's. He said it was the one with blinds.

We landed opposite his door at about four in the afternoon, having come some forty miles this day. From the Piscataquis we had come remarkably and unaccountably quick, probably as fast as the stage or the boat, though the last dozen miles was dead water.

Polis wanted to sell us his canoe, said it would last seven or eight years, or with care, perhaps ten; but we were not ready to buy it.

We stopped for an hour at his house, where my companion shaved with his razor, which he pronounced in very good condition. Mrs. P. wore a hat and had a silver brooch on her breast, but she was not introduced to us. The house was roomy and neat. A large new map of Oldtown and the Indian Island hung on the wall, and a clock opposite to it. Wishing to know when the cars left Oldtown, Polis's son brought one of the last Bangor papers, which I saw was directed to "Joseph Polis," from the office.

This was the last that I saw of Joe Polis. We took

the last train, and reached Bangor that night.

Comments:

Now we can look closer at the canoeing skills of both Joe and Henry:

> *He then wanted to see me paddle in the stern. So, changing paddles, for he had the longer and better one, and turning end for end, he sitting flat on the bottom and I on the crossbar, he began to paddle very hard, trying to turn the canoe, looking over his shoulder and laughing; but finding it in vain, he relaxed his efforts, though we still sped along a mile or two very swiftly. He said that he had no fault to find with my paddling in the stern…*

Each enjoyed it. It is fair to say that each man had considerable canoeing skills and canoeing strength, and each was quite competent in this regard. But there is no doubt as to who the master was considering that he built his own canoe!

This is the end, after 14 days, 11 of them of wilderness interaction, and all just drops? There is no evidence that the two ever interacted again and Thoreau only lived another four (almost five) years. How many people have been influenced by Thoreau with his trip writings is unknown but surely it is vast. Joe Polis likely had a very strong impact as well. It is recorded that Thoreau, as he lay dying was heard to say "moose, Indian".

While starting with a distanced relationship, and entering a mutual contract for learning, sharing the hardships of wilderness travel, and eventually entering some competitive sport, it is strange to see such a casual departure and never meeting again in any way. One might say:

"ver strange."

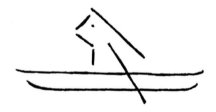

20. *Vignette 6*: Journey continued; following their footsteps and strokes

If the preceding writing has left one wishing for his or her own Thoreau style trip, perhaps on the same path as Polis and Thoreau, be assured that this can be done. Be aware, however, that this is a vastly different process for a beginner or for one with a lot of advanced canoe trip experience. But each can have a very good trip especially if you have a passion for Thoreau's writing and want to relive some of his experiences personally. This is a goal well worth pursuing and can be a life altering experience when you are in the wilderness.

First, take heed of a few basic principles. You can have a lot of fun and great memories in the wilderness; but don't pursue it recklessly. Many do just this and manage to survive ok, but others don't and end up dead, which can readily be avoided. A beginner should not try this trip without a guide, which is just as vital as when Joe Polis guided Thoreau. Be sure your guide also shares your interest and joy in Thoreau's writing and has done the trip before and knows the challenging parts as well. This guide recommendation could just as well apply to seasoned paddlers if a great experience is desired.

If you consider yourself an expert and want to tackle the entire trip without a seasoned guide, be sure to think through the rough spots carefully. Do you want to take the second portage from Umbazookskus to Mud Pond, which Polis described as the wettest portage in Maine, and probably is, or do you want to by-pass this treat? Likewise for the 10-mile portage. Finally, even Joe Polis said he would never do the upper part (*after* Lake Matagamon) of the East Branch again. Yet *he* was able to do it without destroying his canoe. This part might well be reserved for real experts who just thrive on such rough rapids. So planning must be realistic and based on a lot of data; lacking such could have a very bad outcome.

Nonetheless, wonderful trips are possible and a seasoned guide can lead you through all of this. Expect to have various planning and discussion sessions before you ever launch out on your trip; if you are doing the entire trip unguided with a bunch of friends, you will have to spend even more time in preparation in order to have fun and keep safe. No one should be scared away by these cautions, but hopefully be led into a safe and memorable experience.

To help the reader more fully understand the suggested planning, this Maine Guide includes his Planning Notes below by way of illustration.

THOREAU MAINE WOODS CANOEING, LLC.

David Japikse, Registered Maine Guide

Planning Your Thoreau Style 1857 Allagash and East Branch Canoe Trip

Session 1 (1 hour)

1. Introductions and adjusting to trip size and past experiences.
2. Role for strong, experienced trip members and role for new paddlers
3. Safety & PFDs; health and conditioning before the trip; emergency handling
4. Client's expectations; Guide's expectations
5. Fears and anxieties; any scary past experiences? Any concerns?
6. Deer, Moose, Otter, Bear, Raccoon, Lynx, Bobcat, Grouse, Cougar, Turkey, Caribou, Porcupine (*n.b.* several of these do not exist in the Maine Woods)
7. Trip length 4 days to 12 days or other; what can you expect per day?
8. What about bad weather (it does happen) and rest days?
9. What did Thoreau do to enjoy his trip? And you? When raining? Bring a book!

Session 2 (1 hour)

1. Equipment and skills
   a. Canoes
   b. Tents
   c. Clothing; rain gear
   d. Footwear
   e. Packs
   f. Practice paddling and get arms in shape; seats
2. Meals and Cooking
   a. Provided
   b. Most cooking to be done by guide
   c. Breakfast menu; Lunch menu; Dinner menu (Samples)
3. Suggested trip itinerary
4. Preliminary Plan; trip length and starting and end points
5. Fishing is encouraged; get your license before leaving (MOSES)
6. Toileting, washing, diner customs, dish washing – all hands applied
7. Concerns? Safety, first aid.
8. What was Thoreau's low point on his trip? What do you want to avoid on yours?

Session 3 (1 hour)

1. Handling a canoe (30 minute discussion)
   a. Parts of a canoe
   b. Getting in and out; balance; strokes
   c. Our rules of travel
2. Safety at all times – always wear your PFD.
   a. When do accidents happen?
   b. History teaches….
3. Dressing for weather; always work with layers
   a. Sunny – light clothing, sunscreen and hat plus sunglasses
   b. Overcast – warmer layer
   c. Stormy – rain gear, poncho vs raincoat vs bare skin
   d. Footwear – dry shoes and wet shoes, plastic bags?
   e. Sleepwear – dry, comfy; pillow; socks, cap
4. Beating the chills
   a. Body exercise
   b. Warm clothing
   c. Warm fluids
5. How did Thoreau and Polis meet these challenges?

Session 4 (1 hour)

1. Personal Packing List – NO FOOD IN TENTS!
   a. Two changes of clothing plus thermal layers and hat
   b. Sleeping clothes & groundsheet
   c. Water shoes, dry shoes
   d. Pocket knife, dinner drink
   e. Fishing rod
2. Conditioning and Health
   a. Maintain all around good conditioning and health; advise guide of any health issues; will require a health questionnaire to be completed
   b. Develop extra upper body strength; we paddle for hours and switch sides every 5 or 10 minutes; we do take breaks every 90 mins. or so.
3. What did Thoreau pack; what did Joe Polis pack? Comments?
4. Lost person search
   a. Why this?
   b. Guide's duties
   c. Client duties
5. Contrast this contemporary approach to that of Thoreau and Polis

Session 5 (1 hour)

1. Rendezvous before start (housing provided)
2. Pack check
3. Transit to start
4. Group equipment assignments
   a. Tents
   b. Wanigans
   c. Tarp
   d. Paddles
   e. Misc. shovel, axe, etc.
5. Portaging, if elected
   And,
6. Tipping is always your choice (for TMWC, LLC, *all* tips are used *only* for ever better and newer equipment)

Postscript

Thoreau's writing is truly insightful and loaded with complex narratives. I have endeavored to bring this story of a native American guide out of the web of interwoven accounts of diverse observations. Hopefully the details of where they traveled have been accurately puzzled out and recorded as well as some of the wonderful skills that Joe revealed as he led his clients through the wilderness.

I have traveled significant parts of this trail but have avoided the 10-mile portage and some of the worst rapids mentioned herein. I suggest that others might do the same, remembering that Thoreau died just five years after this trip; somewhere, somehow, he contracted tuberculosis and succumbed.

Still, the Thoreau-Polis 1857 trip is a great one. With a little common sense, it can be safely pursued and greatly enjoyed; interested campers can join a trip any summer and probably the same week, a very good season in Maine, that Thoreau and friends took it. If you choose to travel in Henry's footsteps, and venture into the Maine Woods, may you have a wonderful and safe trip filled with many happy memories!

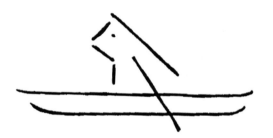

About the Author

Dave Japikse was born in Reading, Pennsylvania, on May 2, 1943, and moved to Bexley, Ohio (near Columbus) in the summer of 1951 at the age of 8. From eight years of age until age 22 he spent one year living in the outdoors hiking, backpacking, canoeing, kayaking, fishing, hunting, and sailing. At age 19 he was solo leading wilderness canoe trips in the Canadian wilderness around Timagami, Ontario. Along the way he became an Eagle Scout, with a gold palm, and developed many hobbies, especially outdoor hobbies. As college years approached, decisions had to be made and a struggled balance between engineering, wilderness sport, and photography ensued.

Dave graduated with a B. Sc. in Engineering Science (essentially mechanical engineering following his dad and grandfather) from Case Institute of Technology in 1965. That summer, he married L. Ellen Drum, his high school sweetheart. This was followed by a M.Sc. and a Ph.D. from Purdue University in the fall of 1968 on an NDEA Title Four scholarship and then into post-Doctoral study as a Fulbright Scholar and an NSF fellow with study in Aachen, Germany. His beloved wilderness seemed far away, but weekend travels helped with much time camping in wilderness areas. Waking up to the cry of a *real* cuckoo bird was special!

The years up to 2022 focused on science and technology with considerable success. Still, many weekends found him in the wilderness either with family, scout units (usually a 3-day trip every 3 weeks and summer trips of about 10 days) as Scout Master and later Post Advisor, plus summer camping with his family. By age 50, he had spent a second-year camping in the wilderness in all seasons; after age 50 he has lost track of how much time has been spent outside!

In 2020 Ellen and Dave began their first annual 10-day trip in the Maine Woods which was very successful. Ellen was closely observing and suggested that Dave really should become a Registered Maine Guide which he did that winter and passed his exam smoothly on April 12th of 2021. At the same time a passion for Thoreau's Maine trips blossomed into this book.

Dave traces much of his canoeing-camping practices back to the Timagami First Nation tribe (Canada) who set the style of wilderness life and practices used during his teenage years.